LIL

A Legend in Seve

BY

FERENC MOLNAR

ENGLISH TEXT BY

BENJAMIN F. GLAZER

SAMUEL FRENCH, INC.
45 WEST 25TH STREET   NEW YORK 10010
7623 SUNSET BOULEVARD HOLLYWOOD 90046
LONDON   TORONTO

Copy of program of the first performance of "Liliom" as produced
at the Garrick Theatre, New York.

THE THEATRE GUILD, INC.

PRESENTS

"LILIOM"

A LEGEND IN SEVEN SCENES AND A PROLOGUE

BY

FERENC MOLNAR

ENGLISH TEXT BY BENJAMIN F. GLAZER

PRODUCED UNDER THE DIRECTION OF FRANK REICHER

CAST OF CHARACTERS

(In the order of their appearance)

MARIE...*Hortense Alden*
JULIE...*Eva Le Gallienne*
MRS. MUSKAT...................................*Helen Westley*
"LILIOM"......................................*Joseph Schildkraut*
FOUR SERVANT GIRLS....................... { *Frances Diamond* *Margaret Mosier* *Anne de Chantal* *Elizabeth Parker* }
POLICEMEN................................ { *Howard Claney* *Lawrence B. Chrow* }
CAPTAIN.......................................*Erskine Sanford*
PLAINCLOTHES MAN..............................*Gerald Stopp*
MOTHER HOLLUNDER..............................*Lilian Kingsbury*
FICSUR, "THE SPARROW".........................*Dudley Digges*
WOLF BEIFELD..................................*Henry Travers*
YOUNG HOLLUNDER...............................*William Franklin*
LINZMAN.......................................*Willard Bowman*
FIRST MOUNTED POLICEMAN.......................*Edgar Stehli*
SECOND MOUNTED POLICEMAN......................*George Frenger*
THE DOCTOR....................................*Robert Babcock*
THE CARPENTER.................................*George Frenger*
FIRST POLICEMAN OF THE BEYOND.................*Erskine Sanford*
SECOND POLICEMAN OF THE BEYOND................*Gerald Stopp*

THE RICHLY DRESSED MAN........................*Edgar Stehli*
THE POORLY DRESSED MAN........................*Philip Wood*
THE OLD GUARD............................*Walton Butterfield*
THE MAGISTRATE...............................*Albert Perry*
LOUISE..*Evelyn Chard*
PEASANTS, TOWNSPEOPLE, ETC.
Lela M. Aultman, Janet Scott, Marion M. Winsten, Katherine Fahnestock, Lillian Tuchman, Ruth L. Cumming, Jacob Weiser, Maurice Somers, John Crump.

PRODUCED UNDER THE DIRECTION OF FRANK REICHER
COSTUMES AND SCENERY DESIGNED BY LEE SIMONSON
TECHNICAL DIRECTOR SHELDON K. VIELE
SCENERY PAINTED BY ROBERT BERGMAN
COSTUMES EXECUTED BY NETTIE DUFF READE
STAGE MANAGER WALTER GEER
ASSISTANT STAGE MANAGER JACOB WEISER
MUSIC ARRANGED BY DEEMS TAYLOR
EXECUTIVE DIRECTOR THERESA HELBURN

SYNOPSIS OF SCENES

PROLOGUE: An amusement park on the outskirts of Budapest.
FIRST SCENE: A lonely place in the park.
SECOND SCENE: The photographic studio of the HOLLUNDERS.
THIRD SCENE: Same as scene two.
FOURTH SCENE: A railroad embankment outside the city.
FIFTH SCENE: Same as scene two.
SIXTH SCENE: A courtroom in the beyond.
SEVENTH SCENE: JULIE's garden.

There are intermissions only after the second and fifth scenes.

STORY OF THE PLAY

Liliom is a shiftless young ne'er-do-well and bully of Budapest. He works intermittently as a barker for a merry-go-round and many servant girls fall victim to his charms. Among these girls is Julie whom he eventually marries. Learning that he is about to become a father Liliom participates in a highway robbery in order to enhance his fortunes. But he is caught in the act and stabs himself rather than submit to arrest. He is tried in the Magistrate's court on high, but they see through him there. They know how he came to beat that girl whom he married down below, how he came to plan the robbery, how he came to kill himself. They know what repentance is in his heart though he is much too cocky to admit it or make any plea for himself. He is sentenced to a term of years in the purifying fires of the penitential plains with the promise that after that sentence has been served he can go back to earth with a chance to do one good deed there.

PROLOGUE

Scene : An amusement park on the outskirts of Budapest on a late afternoon in spring. There are entrances down Right and Left and up Left. A novelty stand above Right entrance ; a merry-go-round up Right Center with barker's stand at the entrance; a fruit stand up Center ; a Punch & Judy show down Left above Left 1 entrance ; a juggler's stand below this entrance. Barkers stand before the booths of the sideshows haranguing the passing crowd. The strident music of a *CALLIOPE* is heard ; laughter, shouts, the scuffle of feet, the signal bells of merry-go-round. CLOWNS circulate among the crowd of PEASANTS, SOLDIERS and WOMEN. The shadow of the horses is seen on the merry-go-round tent.

LILIOM stands at the entrance to the merry-go-round, a cigarette in his mouth, coaxing the people in. The GIRLS regard him with idolizing glances and screech with pleasure as he playfully pushes them through entrance. Now and then some girl's escort resents the familiarity, whereupon LILIOM's demeanor becomes ugly and menacing, and the cowed escort slinks through the entrance behind his girl or contents himself with a muttered resentful comment.

One GIRL hands LILIOM a red carnation; he rewards her with a bow and a smile. When the SOLDIER who accompanies her protests, LILIOM cows him with a fierce glance and a threatening gesture. MARIE and JULIE come out of the crowd and LILIOM favors them with particular notice as they into the merry-go-round.

MRS. MUSKAT comes out of the merry-go-round, bringing LILIOM coffee and rolls. LILIOM mounts the barker's stand at the entrance, where he is elevated over everyone on the stage. Here he begins his harangue. Everybody turns toward him. The other booths are gradually deserted. The tumult makes it impossible for the audience to hear what he is saying, but every now and then some witticism of his provokes a storm of laughter which is audible above the din. Many people enter the merry-go-round. Here and there one catches a phrase "Room for one more on the zebra's back," "Which of you ladies?" "Ten heller for adults, five for children," "Step right up"—

It is growing darker. Lamps are lit. The *WHISTLE* of a distant locomotive is heard. Suddenly the tumult ceases, the *LIGHTS* go out, and the Curtain falls in darkness.

END OF PROLOGUE

SCENE ONE

SCENE: *A lonely place in the park, half hidden by trees and shrubbery. There are entrances Right and Left. Under a flowering acacia tree stands a painted wooden bench Center. From the distance, faintly, comes the TUMULT of the amusement park. The CALLIOPE plays. It is the sunset of the same day.*
When the Curtain rises the stage is empty.
MARIE *enters quickly Left, pauses at Center, and looks back.*

MARIE. Julie, Julie! [*There is no answer.*] Do you hear me, Julie? Let her be! Come on. Let her be. [*Starts to go back a step to Left Center.*]

JULIE. [*Enters Left, looks back angrily. Crosses to* MARIE.] Did you ever hear of such a thing? What's the matter with the woman anyway?

MARIE. [*Looking back again.*] Here she comes again.

JULIE. Let her come. I didn't do anything to her. All of a sudden she comes up to me and begins to raise a row.

MARIE. Here she is. Come on, let's run. [*Takes* JULIE's *hand. Tries to urge her off.*]

JULIE. [*Center.*] Run? I should say not. What would I want to run for? I'm not afraid of her.

MARIE. [*Right of* JULIE.] Oh, come on. She'll only start a fight.

7

JULIE. I'm going to stay right here. Let her *start* a fight.

MRS. MUSKAT. [*Entering Left to Center.*] What do you want to run away for? [*To* JULIE.] Don't worry. I won't eat you. But there's one thing I want to tell you, my dear. Don't let me catch you in my carousel again. I stand for a whole lot, I have to in my business. It makes no difference to me whether my customers are ladies or the likes of you—as long as they pay their money. But when a girl misbehaves herself on my carousel—out she goes. Do you understand?

JULIE. Are you talking to me?

MRS. MUSKAT. Yes, you! You—*chamber-maid,* you! In my carousel—

JULIE. Who did anything in your old carousel? I paid my fare and took my seat and never said a word, except to my friend here.

MARIE. No, she never opened her mouth. Liliom came over to her of his own accord.

MRS. MUSKAT. It's all the same. I'm not going to get in trouble with the police, and lose my license on account of you—you shabby kitchen-maid!

JULIE. Shabby yourself.

MRS. MUSKAT. You stay out of my carousel! Letting my barker fool with you! Aren't you ashamed of yourself?

JULIE. What? What did you say?

MRS. MUSKAT. I suppose you think I have no eyes in my head. I see everything that goes on in my carousel. During the whole ride she let Liliom fool with her—the shameless hussy!

JULIE. He did not fool with me! I don't let any man fool with me!

MRS. MUSKAT. He *leaned* against you all through the ride!

JULIE. He leaned against the panther. He always leans against something, doesn't he? Everybody leans where he wants. I couldn't tell him not to lean, if he always leans, could I? But he didn't lay a hand on me.

MRS. MUSKAT. Oh, didn't he? And I suppose he didn't put his hand around your waist, either?

MARIE. And if he did? What of it?

MRS. MUSKAT. You hold your tongue! No one's asking you—just you keep out of it.

JULIE. He put his arm around my waist—just the same as he does to all the girls. He always does that.

MRS. MUSKAT. I'll teach him not to do it any more, my dear. No carryings on in my carousel! If you are looking for that sort of thing, you'd better go to the circus! You'll find lots of soldiers there to carry on with!

JULIE. You keep your soldiers for yourself!

MARIE. Soldiers! As if we wanted soldiers!

MRS. MUSKAT. Well, I only want to tell you this, my dear, so that we understand each other perfectly. If you ever stick your nose in my carousel again, you'll wish you hadn't! I'm not going to lose my license on account of the likes of you! People who don't know how to behave, have got to stay out!

JULIE. You're wasting your breath. If I feel like riding

on your carousel I'll play my ten heller and I'll ride. I'd like to see anyone try to stop me!

MRS. MUSKAT. Just come and try it, my dear—just come and try it.

MARIE. We'll see what'll happen.

MRS. MUSKAT. Yes, you will see something happen that never happened before in this park. [*Starts; gets to Left Center; stops.*]

JULIE. Perhaps you think you could throw me out!

MRS. MUSKAT. I'm sure of it, my dear.

JULIE. And suppose I'm stronger than you?

MRS. MUSKAT. I'd think twice before I'd dirty my hands on a common servant girl. I'll have Liliom throw you out. He knows how to handle your kind.

JULIE. You think Liliom would throw me out.

MRS. MUSKAT. Yes, my dear, so fast that you won't know what happened to you!

JULIE. He'd throw me—

[*Stops suddenly, for* MRS. MUSKAT *has turned away.* BOTH *look off stage until* LILIOM *enters Left, surrounded by four giggling* SERVANT GIRLS.]

LILIOM. Go away! Stop following me, or I'll smack your face!

A LITTLE SERVANT GIRL. Well, give me back my handkerchief.

LILIOM. Go on now—

THE FOUR SERVANT GIRLS. [*Simultaneously.*] What do

you think of him?—My handkerchief!—Give it back to her!—That's a nice thing to do!

THE LITTLE SERVANT GIRL. [*To* MRS. MUSKAT.] Please, lady, make him—

MRS. MUSKAT. Oh, shut up!

LILIOM. Will you get out of here? [*Makes a threatening gesture, slapping one of them behind.*
[THE FOUR SERVANT GIRLS *exit Left in voluble but fearful haste.*]

MRS. MUSKAT. What have you been doing now?

LILIOM. [*Crossing to Center.*] None of your business. [*Glances at* JULIE.] Have you been starting with her again?

JULIE. Mister Liliom, please—

LILIOM. [*Steps threateningly toward her.*] Don't yell!

JULIE. [*Timidly.*] I didn't yell.

LILIOM. Well, don't. [*To* MRS. MUSKAT.] What's the matter? What has she done to you?

MRS. MUSKAT. What has she done? She's been impudent to me. Just as impudent as she could be! I put her out of the carousel. Take a good look at this innocent thing, Liliom. She's never to be allowed in my carousel again!

LILIOM. [*To* JULIE.] You heard that. Run home, now. [*Turns up Left Center.*]

MARIE. Come on. Don't waste your time with such people. [*Tries to lead* JULIE *away to Right.*]

JULIE. No, I won't—

MRS. MUSKAT. If she ever comes again, you're not to let

her in. And if she gets in before you see her, throw her out. Understand?

LILIOM. [*Coming down.*] What has she done, anyhow?

JULIE. [*Agitated and very earnest.*] Mister Liliom—tell me please—honest and truly—if I come into the carousel, will you throw me out?

MRS. MUSKAT. Of course he'll throw you out.

MARIE. She wasn't talking to you.

JULIE. Tell me straight to my face, Mister Liliom, would you throw me out?

[*They face each other. There is a brief pause.*]

LILIOM. Yes, little girl, if there was a reason—but if there was no reason, why should I throw you out?

MARIE. [*To* MRS. MUSKAT.] There, you see!

JULIE. Thank you, Mister Liliom.

MRS. MUSKAT. And I tell you again, if this little slut dares to set her foot in my carousel, she's to be thrown out! I'll stand for no indecency in my establishment.

LILIOM. What do you mean—indecency?

MRS. MUSKAT. I saw it all. There's no use denying it.

JULIE. She says you put your arm around my waist.

LILIOM. Me?

MRS. MUSKAT. Yes, you! I saw you. Don't play the innocent.

LILIOM. Here's something new! I'm not to put my arm

around a girl's waist any more! I suppose I'm to ask your permission before I touch another girl!

MRS. MUSKAT. You can touch as many girls as you want and as often as you want—for my part you can go as far as you like with any of them—but not this one—I permit no indecency in my carousel.

[*There is a long pause.*]

LILIOM. [*To* MRS. MUSKAT.] And now I'll ask you please to shut your mouth.

MRS. MUSKAT. What?

LILIOM. [*A step to her.*] Shut your mouth quick, and go back to your carousel.

MRS. MUSKAT. [*Retreating a step.*] What?

LILIOM. What did she do to you, anyhow? [*Turns up Left Center.*] Tryin' to start a fight with a little pigeon like that [*Faces* MRS. MUSKAT.] just because I touched her? [*Crosses down Center.*] You come to the carousel as often as you want to, little girl. Come every afternoon, and sit on the panther's back, and if you haven't got the price, Liliom will pay for you. And if anyone dares to bother you, you come and tell *me*.

MRS. MUSKAT. You reprobate!

LILIOM. Old witch!

JULIE. Thank you, Mister Liliom.

MRS. MUSKAT. [*A step Center.*] You seem to think that I can't throw *you* out, too. What's the reason I can't? Because you are the best barker in the park? Well, you are very much mistaken. In fact, you can consider yourself thrown out already. You're discharged!

LILIOM. Very good. [*Sits on bench.*]

MRS. MUSKAT. [*Weakening a little.*] I can discharge you any time I feel like it.

LILIOM. Very good, you feel like discharging me. I'm discharged. That settles it.

MRS. MUSKAT. Playing the high and mighty, are you? Conceited pig! Good-for-nothing!

LILIOM. You said you'd throw me out, didn't you? Well, that suits me; I'm thrown out.

MRS. MUSKAT. [*Softening.*] Do you have to take up every word I say?

LILIOM. It's all right; it's all settled. I'm a good-for-nothing. And a conceited pig. And I'm discharged.

MRS. MUSKAT. Do you want to ruin my business?

LILIOM. A good-for-nothing? Now I know! And I'm discharged! Very good.

MRS. MUSKAT. You're a devil, you are—and that woman—

LILIOM. [*Rising.*] Keep away from her!

MRS. MUSKAT. I'll get Hollinger to give you such a beating that you'll hear all the angels sing—and it won't be the first time, either.

LILIOM. [*A step to* MRS. MUSKAT.] Get out of here. I'm discharged. And you get out of here. [*Turns Center.*]

JULIE. [*Timidly.*] Mister Liliom, if she's willing to say that she hasn't discharged you—

LILIOM. You keep out of this.

JULIE. [*Timidly.*] I don't want this to happen on account of me.

LILIOM. [*To* MRS. MUSKAT, *pointing to* JULIE.] Apologize to her!

MARIE. A-ha!

MRS. MUSKAT. Apologize? To who?

LILIOM. To this little pigeon. [*Pause. Then threateningly.*] Well—are you going to do it?

MRS. MUSKAT. If you give me this whole park on a silver plate, and all the gold of the Rothschilds on top of it— I'd—I'd— Let her dare to come into my carousel again and she'll get thrown out so hard that she'll see stars in daylight!

LILIOM. In that case, dear lady [*takes off his cap with a flourish*], you are respectfully requested to get out o' here as fast as your legs will carry you—I never beat up a woman yet—except that Holzer woman who I sent to the hospital for three weeks—but—if you don't get out o' here this minute, and let this little squab be, I'll give you the prettiest slap in the jaw you ever had in your life. [*Advances to her.*]

MRS. MUSKAT. [*Retreating Left a step.*] Very good, my son. Now you *can* go to the devil. Good-bye. You're discharged, and you needn't try to come back, either. [*She spits at him and exits Left.*]

MARIE. [*Pause. Crosses to* LILIOM. *With grave concern.*] Mister Liliom—

LILIOM. Don't you pity me or I'll give *you* a slap in the jaw. [*Crosses to Center. To* JULIE.] And don't you pity me, either. [*Starts to turn Left.*]

JULIE. [*In alarm.*] I don't pity you, Mister Liliom.

LILIOM. [*Stops.*] You're a liar, you *are* pitying me. I can see it in your face. [*Paces Left Center and back.*] You're thinking, now that Madame Muskat has thrown him out, Liliom will have to go begging. Huh! Look at me. I'm big enough to get along without a Madame Muskat. I have been thrown out of better jobs than hers.

JULIE. What will you do now, Mister Liliom?

LILIOM. Now? First of all, I'll go and get myself—a glass of beer. You see, when something happens to annoy me, I always drink a glass of beer.

JULIE. Then you *are* annoyed about losing your job.

LILIOM. No, only about where I'm going to get the beer.

MARIE. Well—eh—

LILIOM. Well—eh—what?

MARIE. Well—eh—are you going to stay with us, Mister Liliom?

LILIOM. Will you pay for the beer? [MARIE *looks doubtful; he turns to* JULIE.] Will you? [*She does not answer.*] How much money have you got?

JULIE. [*Bashfully.*] Eight heller.

LILIOM. And you? [MARIE *casts down her eyes and does not reply.* LILIOM *continues sternly.*] I asked you how much you've got? [MARIE *begins to weep softly.*] I understand. Well, you needn't cry about it. You girls stay here, while I go back to the carousel and get my clothes and things. And when I come back, we'll go to the Hungarian beer-garden. It's all right, I'll pay. Keep your money. [*He exits Left.*]

[MARIE *and* JULIE *stand silent, watching him until he has gone.*]

MARIE. Are you sorry for him?

JULIE. Are you?

MARIE. Yes, a little. Why are you looking after him in that funny way? [*Crosses to Center.*]

JULIE. [*Sits on bench.*] Nothing—except I'm sorry he lost his job.

MARIE. [*Sits beside her with a touch of pride.*] It was on our account he lost his job. Because he's fallen in love with you.

JULIE. He hasn't at all.

MARIE. [*Confidently.*] Oh, yes! he is in love with you. [*Hesitantly, romantically.*] There is someone in love with me, too.

JULIE. There is? Who?

MARIE. I—I never mentioned it before, because you hadn't a lover of your own—but now you have—and I'm free to speak. [*Very grandiloquently.*] My heart has found its mate.

JULIE. You're only making it up.

MARIE. No, it's true—my heart's true love—

JULIE. Who? Who is he?

MARIE. A soldier.

JULIE. What kind of a soldier?

MARIE. I don't know. Just a soldier. Are there different kinds?

JULIE. Many different kinds. There are hussars, artillerymen, engineers, infantry—that's the kind that walks —and—

MARIE. How can you tell which is which?

JULIE. By their uniforms.

MARIE. [*After trying to puzzle it out.*] The conductors on the street cars—are they soldiers?

JULIE. Certainly not. They're conductors.

MARIE. Well, they have uniforms.

JULIE. But they don't carry swords or guns.

MARIE. Oh! [*Thinks it over again; then.*] Well, policemen—are they?

JULIE. [*With a touch of exasperation.*] Are they what?

MARIE. Soldiers.

JULIE. Certainly not. They're just policemen.

MARIE. [*Triumphantly.*] But they have uniforms—and they carry weapons, too.

JULIE. You're just as dumb as you can be. You don't go by their uniforms.

MARIE. But you said—

JULIE. No, I didn't. A letter-carrier wears a uniform, too, but that doesn't make him a soldier.

MARIE. But if he carried a gun or a sword, would he be—

JULIE. No, he'd still be a letter-carrier. You can't go by guns or swords, either.

MARIE. Well, if you don't go by the uniforms or the weapons, what *do* you go by?

JULIE. By— [*Tries to put it into words; fails; then breaks off suddenly.*] Oh, you'll get to know when you've lived in the city long enough. You're nothing but a country girl. When you've lived in the city a year, like I have, you'll know all about it.

MARIE. [*Half angrily.*] Well, how *do* you know when *you* see a real soldier?

JULIE. By one thing.

MARIE. What?

JULIE. One thing— [*She pauses.* MARIE *starts to cry.*] Oh, what are you crying about?

MARIE. Because you're making fun of me.—You're a city girl, and I'm just fresh from the country—and how am I expected to know a soldier when I see one?—You, you ought to tell me, instead of making fun of me—

JULIE. All right. Listen then, cry-baby. There's only one way to tell a soldier: by his salute! That's the only way.

MARIE. [*Joyfully; with a sigh of relief.*] Ah—that's good.

JULIE. What?

MARIE. I say—it's all right then—because Wolf—Wolf — [JULIE *laughs derisively.*] Wolf—that's his name. [*She weeps again.*]

JULIE. Crying again? What now?

MARIE. You're making fun of me again.

JULIE. I'm not. But when you say, "Wolf—Wolf—" like that, I have to laugh, don't I? [*Archly.*] What's his name again?

MARIE. I won't tell you.

JULIE. All right. If you won't say it, then he's no soldier.

MARIE. I'll say it.

JULIE. Go on.

MARIE. No, I won't. [*She weeps again.*]

JULIE. Then he's not a soldier. I guess he's a letter-carrier—

MARIE. No—no—I'd rather say it.

JULIE. Well, then.

MARIE. [*Giggling.*] But you mustn't look at me. You look the other way, and I'll say it. [JULIE *looks away.* MARIE *can hardly restrain her own laughter.*] Wolf! [*She laughs.*] That's his real name. Wolf, Wolf, Soldier— Wolf!

JULIE. What kind of a uniform does he wear?

MARIE. Red.

JULIE. Red trousers?

MARIE. No.

JULIE. Red coat?

MARIE. No.

JULIE. What then?

MARIE. [*Triumphantly.*] His cap!

JULIE. [After a long pause.] He's just a porter, you dunce. Red cap—that's a porter—and he doesn't carry a gun or a sword, either.

MARIE. [*Triumphantly.*] But he salutes. You said yourself that was the only way to tell a soldier—

JULIE. He doesn't salute at all. He only greets people—

MARIE. He salutes me. And if his name *is* Wolf, that doesn't prove he ain't a soldier—he salutes, and he wears a red cap and he stands on guard all day long outside a big building—

JULIE. What does he do there?

MARIE. [*Seriously.*] He spits.

JULIE. [*With contempt.*] He's nothing—nothing but a common porter.

MARIE. What's Liliom?

JULIE. [*Indignantly.*] Why speak of him? What has he to do with me?

MARIE. The same as Wolf has to do with me. If you can talk to me like that about Wolf, I can talk to you about Liliom.

JULIE. He's nothing to me. He put his arm around me in the carousel. I couldn't tell him not to put his arm around me after he had done it, could I?

MARIE. I suppose you didn't like him to do it?

JULIE. No.

MARIE. Then why are you waiting for him? Why don't you go home?

JULIE. Why—eh—he *said* we were to wait for him.

[LILIOM *enters Left. There is a long silence.*]

LILIOM. Are you still here? What are you waiting for?

MARIE. You told us to wait.

LILIOM. Must you always interfere? No one is talking to you.

MARIE. You asked us—why we—

LILIOM. Will you keep your mouth shut? What do you suppose I want with two of you? I meant that one of you was to wait. The other can go home.

MARIE. All right.

JULIE. All right.

[*Neither starts to go.*]

LILIOM. One of you goes home. [*To* MARIE.] Where do you work?

MARIE. At the Breier's, Damjanovitsch Street, Number 20.

LILIOM. And you?

JULIE. I work there, too.

LILIOM. Well, one of you goes home. Which of you wants to stay. [*There is no answer.*] Come on, speak up, which of you stays?

MARIE. [*Officiously.*] She'll lose her job if she stays.

LILIOM. Who will?

MARIE. Julie. She has to be back by seven o'clock.

LILIOM. Is that true? Will they discharge you if you're not back on time?

JULIE. Yes.

LILIOM. Well, wasn't I discharged?

JULIE. Yes— you were discharged, too.

MARIE. Julie, shall I go?

JULIE. I—can't tell you what to do.

MARIE. All right—stay if you like.

LILIOM. You'll be discharged if you do?

MARIE. Shall I go, Julie?

JULIE. [*Embarrassed.*] Why do you keep asking me that?

MARIE. You know best what to do. [*Rises. Crosses to Right Center.*]

JULIE. [*Profoundly moved; slowly.*] It's all right, Marie, you can go home.

MARIE. [*Exits Right reluctantly, but comes back, and says uncertainly.*] Good-night. [*She waits a moment to see if* JULIE *will follow her.* JULIE *does not move.* MARIE *exits Right.*]

[*Meantime it has grown quite dark. During the following scene the gas-lamps far in the distance are lighted one by one.* LILIOM *and* JULIE *sit on the bench. From afar, very faintly, comes the music of a CALLIOPE. But the music is intermittently heard; now it breaks off, now it resumes again, as if it came down on a fitful wind. Blending with it are the SOUNDS of human voices, now loud, now soft; the blare of a toy trumpet; the confused noises of the show-booths. It grows progressively darker until the end of the scene. There is no moonlight. The spring iridescence glows in the deep blue sky.*]

LILIOM. Now we're both discharged. [*She does not answer. From now on they speak gradually lower and lower until the end of the scene, which is played almost in whispers. Whistles softly, then.*] Have you had your supper?

JULIE. No.

LILIOM. Want to go eat something at the Garden?

JULIE. No.

LILIOM. Anywhere else?

JULIE. No.

LILIOM. [*Whistles softly, then.*] You don't come to this park very often, do you? I've only seen you three times. Been here oftener than that?

JULIE. Oh, yes.

LILIOM. Did you see me?

JULIE. Yes.

LILIOM. And did you know I was Liliom?

JULIE. They told me.

LILIOM. [*Whistles softly, then.*] Have you got a sweetheart?

JULIE. No.

LILIOM. Don't lie to me.

JULIE. I haven't. If I had, I'd tell you. I've never had one.

LILIOM. What an awful liar you are. I've got a good mind to go away and leave you here.

JULIE. I've never had one.

LILIOM. Tell that to someone else.

JULIE. [*Reproachfully.*] Why do you insist I have?

LILIOM. Because you stayed here with me the first time I asked you to. You know your way around, you do.

JULIE. No, I don't, Mister Liliom.

LILIOM. I suppose you'll tell me you don't know why you're sitting here—like this, in the dark, alone with me— You wouldn't 'a' stayed so quick, if you hadn't done it before—with some soldier, maybe. This isn't the first time. You wouldn't have been so ready to stay if it was—what *did* you stay for, anyhow?

JULIE. So you wouldn't be left alone.

LILIOM. Alone! God, you're dumb! I don't need to be alone. I can have all the girls I want. Not only servant girls like you, but cooks and governesses, even French girls. I could have twenty of them if I wanted to.

JULIE. I know, Mr. Liliom.

LILIOM. What do you know?

JULIE. That all the girls are in love with you. But that's not why *I* stayed. I stayed because you've been so good to me.

LILIOM. Well, then you can go home.

JULIE. I don't want to go home now.

LILIOM. And what if I go away and leave you sitting here?

JULIE. If you did, I wouldn't go home.

LILIOM. Do you know what you remind me of? A sweetheart I had once— I'll tell you how I met her— One night, at closing time, we had put out the lights in the carousel, and just as I was—

[*Police WHISTLE blows off Right and he is interrupted by the entrance of two plainclothes* POLICEMEN *from Right. They take their stations on either side of the bench.*]

FIRST POLICEMAN. [*To Right of bench.*] What are you doing there?

LILIOM. Me?

SECOND POLICEMAN. [*To Left of bench.*] Stand up when you're spoken to! [*He taps* LILIOM *imperatively on the shoulder.*]

[LILIOM *rises.*]

FIRST POLICEMAN. What's your name?

LILIOM. Andreas Zavoczki.

[JULIE *begins to weep softly.*]

SECOND POLICEMAN. Stop your bawling. We're not goin' to eat you. We are only making our rounds.

FIRST POLICEMAN. See that he doesn't get away. [THE SECOND POLICEMAN *steps closer to* LILIOM.] What's your business?

LILIOM. Barker and bouncer.

SECOND POLICEMAN. They call him Liliom, Chief. We've had him up a couple of times.

FIRST POLICEMAN. So that's who you are! Who do you work for now?

LILIOM. I work for the widow Muskat.

FIRST POLICEMAN. What are you hanging around here for?

LILIOM. We're just sitting here—me and this girl.

FIRST POLICEMAN. Your sweetheart?

LILIOM. No.

FIRST POLICEMAN. [*To* JULIE.] And who are you?

JULIE. Julie Zeller.

FIRST POLICEMAN. Servant girl?

JULIE. Maid of All Work for Mister Georg Breier, Number 20 Damjanovitsch Street.

FIRST POLICEMAN. Show your hands.

SECOND POLICEMAN. [*After examining* JULIE's *hand*.] Servant girl.

FIRST POLICEMAN. Why aren't you at home? What are you doing out here with him?

JULIE. This is my day out, sir.

FIRST POLICEMAN. It would be better for you if you didn't spend it sitting around with a fellow like this.

SECOND POLICEMAN. They'll be disappearing in the bushes as soon as we turn our backs.

FIRST POLICEMAN. He's only after your money. We know this fine fellow. He picks up you silly servant girls and takes what money you have. Tomorrow you'll probably be coming around to report him. If you do, I'll throw you out.

JULIE. I haven't any money, sir.

FIRST POLICEMAN. Do you hear that, Liliom?

LILIOM. I'm not looking for her money.

SECOND POLICEMAN. Keep your mouth shut.

FIRST POLICEMAN. It is my duty to warn you, my child, what kind of company you're in. He makes a specialty of servant girls. That's why he works in a carousel. He gets hold of a girl, promises to marry her, then he takes her money and her ring.

JULIE. But I haven't got a ring.

SECOND POLICEMAN. You're not to talk unless you're asked a question.

FIRST POLICEMAN. You be thankful that I'm warning you. It's nothing to me what you do. I'm not your father, thank God. But I'm telling you what kind of a fellow he is. By tomorrow morning you'll be coming around to us to report him. Now you be sensible and go home. You needn't be afraid of him. This officer will take you home if you're afraid.

JULIE. [*Rises and hesitates.*] Do I *have* to go?

FIRST POLICEMAN. No, you don't *have* to go.

JULIE. Then I'll stay, sir.

FIRST POLICEMAN. Well, you've been warned.

JULIE. Yes, sir. Thank you, sir.

FIRST POLICEMAN. Come on, Berkovics.

[*The* POLICEMEN *exit Left.* JULIE *and* LILIOM *sit on the bench again. There is a brief pause.*]

JULIE. Well, and what then?

LILIOM. [*Fails to understand.*] Huh?

JULIE. You were beginning to tell me a story.

LILIOM. Me?

JULIE. Yes, about a sweetheart. You said, one night, just as they were putting out the lights of the carousel— That's as far as you got.

LILIOM. Oh, yes, yes, just as the lights were going out, someone came along—a little girl with a big shawl— you know— She came—eh—from— Say—tell me— ain't you—that is, ain't you at all—afraid of me? The officer told you what kind of a fellow I am—and that I'd take your money away from you—

JULIE. You couldn't take it away—I haven't got any. But if I had—I'd—I'd give it to you—I'd give it all to you.

LILIOM. You would?

JULIE. If you asked me for it.

LILIOM. Have you ever had a fellow you gave money to?

JULIE. No.

LILIOM. Haven't you ever had a sweetheart?

JULIE. No.

LILIOM. Someone you used to go walking with. You've had one like that?

JULIE. Yes.

LILIOM. A soldier?

JULIE. He came from the same village I did.

LILIOM. That's what all the soldiers say. Where *do* you come from, anyway?

JULIE. Not far from here.

[*There is a pause.*]

LILIOM. Were you in love with him?

JULIE. Why do you keep asking me that all the time, Mister Liliom? I wasn't in love with him. We only went walking together.

LILIOM. Where did you walk?

JULIE. In the park.

LILIOM. And your virtue? Where did you lose that?

JULIE. I haven't got any virtue.

LILIOM. Well, you had once.

JULIE. No, I never had. I'm a respectable girl.

LILIOM. Yes, but you gave the soldier something.

JULIE. Why do you question me like that, Mister Liliom?

LILIOM. Did you give him something?

JULIE. You have to. But I didn't love him.

LILIOM. Do you love me?

JULIE. No, Mister Liliom.

LILIOM. Then why do you stay here with me?

JULIE. Um—nothing.

[*There is a pause. The MUSIC from afar is plainly heard.*]

LILIOM. Want to dance?

JULIE. No. I have to be very careful.

LILIOM. Of what?

JULIE. My—character.

LILIOM. Why?

JULIE. Because I'm never going to marry. If I was going to marry, it would be different. Then I wouldn't need to worry so much about my character. It doesn't make any difference if you're married. But I shan't marry—and that's why I've got to take care to be a respectable girl.

LILIOM. Suppose I were to say to you—I'll marry you.

JULIE. You?

LILIOM. That frightens you, doesn't it? You're thinking of what the officer said and you're afraid.

JULIE. No, I'm not, Mister Liliom. I don't pay any attention to what he said.

LILIOM. But you wouldn't dare to marry anyone like me, would you?

JULIE. I know that—that—if I loved anyone—it wouldn't make any difference to me what he—even if I died for it.

LILIOM. But you wouldn't marry a rough guy like me—that is,—eh—if you loved me—

JULIE. Yes, I would—if I loved you, Mister Liliom.

[*There is a pause.*]

LILIOM. [*Whispers.*] Well,—you just said—didn't you? —that you don't love me. Well, why don't you go home then?

JULIE. It's too late now, they'd all be asleep.

LILIOM. Locked out?

JULIE. Certainly.

[*They are silent a while.*]

LILIOM. I think—that even a low-down good-for-nothing—can make a man of himself.

JULIE. Certainly.

[*They are silent again.*]

LILIOM. Are you hungry?

JULIE. No.

[*Another pause. The CALLIOPE stops.*]

LILIOM. Suppose—you had some money—and I took it from you?

                              [*WARN CURTAIN*]

JULIE. Then you could take it, that's all.

LILIOM. [*After another brief silence.*] All I have to do
—is go back to her—that Muskat woman—she'll be
glad to get me back—then I'd be earning my wages
again.

[*She is silent. The twilight folds darker about them.*]

JULIE. [*After a pause. Very softly.*] Don't go back—
to her—

[*Pause.*]

LILIOM. There are a lot of acacia trees around here.

[*Pause.*]

JULIE. Don't go back to her—

[*Pause.*]

LILIOM. She'd take me back the minute I asked her. I
know why—she knows, too—

[*Pause.*]

JULIE. I can smell them, too—acacia blossoms—

[*There is a pause. Some blossoms drift down from the
tree-top to the bench.* LILIOM *picks one up and smells it.*]

LILIOM. White acacias!

JULIE. [*After a brief pause.*] The wind brings them
down.

[*They are silent. The MERRY-GO-ROUND is heard
in the distance. There is a long pause before*

THE CURTAIN FALLS

SCENE TWO

SCENE: *Photographer's studio operated by the* HOL-LUNDERS *on the fringe of the park. It is a dilapidated hovel. General entrance back Center. Back Right Center is a hole in the fence. The door to the kitchen is up Right. A brown-curtained entrance to* JULIE'S *and* LILIOM'S *room is down Right. The door to the dark room is up Left. There is a washstand and bucket down Right; a table and two chairs at Right Center; a chair Left, a couch against the fence back Right Center; a photographer's screen Right of couch; a tripod and camera over Left.*

It is forenoon. When the Curtain rises, MARIE *Left of table and* JULIE *Right of table are discovered.*

MARIE. And *he* beat up Hollinger?

JULIE. Yes, he gave him an awful licking.

MARIE. But Hollinger is bigger than he is.

JULIE. He licked him just the same. It isn't size that counts, you know, it's cleverness. And Liliom's awful quick.

MARIE. And then he was arrested?

JULIE. Yes, they arrested him, but they let him go the next day. That makes twice in the two months we've been living here that Liliom's been arrested and let go again.

MARIE. Why do they let him go?

JULIE. Because he is innocent.

[MOTHER HOLLUNDER, *a very old woman, sharp-tongued, but in reality quite warm-hearted beneath her formidable exterior, enters Center from Right, carrying a few sticks of firewood, and scolding, half to herself.*]

MOTHER HOLLUNDER. Always wanting something, but never willing to work for it. He won't work, and he won't steal, but he'll use up a poor old widow's last bit of firewood. He'll do that cheerfully enough! A big, strong lout like that lying around all day resting his lazy bones! He ought to be ashamed to look decent people in the face.

JULIE. I'm sorry, Mother Hollunder—

MOTHER HOLLUNDER. Sorry! Better be sorry the lazy good-for-nothing ain't in jail where he belongs instead of in the way of honest, hard-working people. [*She exits up Right.*]

MARIE. Who's that?

JULIE. Mrs. Hollunder—my aunt. This is her studio. She lets us live here for nothing. [*Points to down Right door.*]

MARIE. What's she fetching the wood for?

JULIE. She brings us everything we need. If it weren't for her I don't know what would become of us. She's a good-hearted soul even if her tongue is sharp.

MARIE. [*Shyly.*] Do you know—I've found out. He's not a soldier.

JULIE. Do you still see him?

MARIE. Oh, yes.

JULIE. Often?

MARIE. Very often. He's asked me——

JULIE. To marry you?

MARIE. To marry me.

JULIE. You see—that proves he isn't a soldier.

[*There is another pause.*]

MARIE. [*Abashed, yet a bit boastfully.*] Do you know what I'm doing—I'm flirting with him.

JULIE. Flirting?

MARIE. Yes. He asks me to go to the park—and I say I can't go. Then he coaxes me, and promises me a new scarf for my head if I go. But I don't go—even then. So then he walks all the way home with me—and I bid him good-night at the door.

JULIE. Is that what you call flirting?

MARIE. Um-hm! It's sinful, but it's so *thrilling*.

JULIE. Do you ever quarrel?

MARIE. [*Grandly.*] Only when our passionate love surges up.

JULIE. Your passionate love?

MARIE. Yes. He takes my hand and we walk along together. Then he wants to swing hands, but I won't let him. I say: "Don't swing my hand"; and he says,

"Don't be so stubborn." And then he tries to swing my
hand again, but still I don't let him. And for a long time
I don't let him—until in the end I let him. Then we
walk along swinging hands—up and down, up and
down—just like this. *That* is passionate love. It's sinful, but it's awfully *thrilling*.

JULIE. You're happy, aren't you?

MARIE. Happier than—anything— But the most beauti-
ful thing on earth is ideal love.

JULIE. What kind is that?

MARIE. Daylight comes about three in the morning this
time of the year. When we've been up that long we're
all through with flirting and passionate love—and then
our ideal love comes to the surface. It comes like this:
I'll be sitting on the bench and Wolf, he holds my hand
tight—and he puts his cheek against my cheek and we
don't talk—we just sit there very quiet.—And after a
while he gets sleepy, and his head sinks down, and he
falls asleep—but even in his sleep he holds tight to my
hand. And I—I sit perfectly still just looking around
me and taking long, deep breaths—for by that time it's
morning and the trees and flowers are fresh with dew.
But Wolf doesn't smell anything because he's so fast
asleep. And I get awfully sleepy myself, but I don't
sleep. And we sit like that for a long time. That is ideal
love—

[*There is a long pause.* MOTHER HOLLUNDER *enters
with water-pot, grumbling as she exits Center to Right.*]

JULIE. [*Regretfully; uneasily.*] He went out last night
and he hasn't come home yet.

MARIE. Here are sixteen kreuzer. It was supposed to be carfare to take my young lady to the conservatory—eight there and eight back—but I made her walk. Here —save it with the rest.

JULIE. [*Takes money.*] This makes three gulden, forty-six.

MARIE. Three gulden, forty-six.

JULIE. He won't work at all.

MARIE. Too lazy?

JULIE. No. He never learned a trade, you see, and he can't just go and be a day-laborer—so he just does nothing.

MARIE. That ain't right.

JULIE. No. Have the Breiers got a new maid yet?

MARIE. They've had three since you left. You know, Wolf's going to take a new job. He's going to work for the city. He'll get rent free, too.

JULIE. He won't go back to work at the carousel either. I ask him why, but he won't tell me— Last Monday he hit me.

MARIE. Did you hit him back?

JULIE. No.

MARIE. Why don't you leave him?

JULIE. I don't want to.

MARIE. I would. I'd leave him.

[*There is a strained silence.*]

MOTHER HOLLUNDER. [*Enters Center from Right, carrying a pot of water; muttering aloud*] He can play cards, all right. He can fight, too; and take money from poor servant girls. And the police turn their heads the other way— The carpenter was here.

JULIE. Is that water for the soup?

MOTHER HOLLUNDER. The carpenter was here. There's a *man* for you! Dark, handsome, lots of hair, a respectable widower with two children—and money, and a good paying business.

JULIE. [*To* MARIE.] It's three gulden, sixty-six, not forty-six.

MARIE. Yes, that's what I make it—sixty-six.

MOTHER HOLLUNDER. He wants to take her out of this and marry her. This is the fifth time he's been here. He has two children, but—

JULIE. Please don't bother, Aunt Hollunder, I'll get the water myself.

MOTHER HOLLUNDER. He's waiting outside now.

JULIE. Send him away.

MOTHER HOLLUNDER. He'll only come back again—and first thing you know that vagabond will get jealous and there'll be a fight. [*Starts up Right, muttering.*] Oh, he's ready enough to fight, he is. Strike a poor little girl like that! Ought to be ashamed of himself! And the police just let him go on doing as he pleases. [*Still scolding, she exits up Right.*]

MARIE. A carpenter wants to marry you?

JULIE. Yes.

MARIE. Why don't you?

JULIE. Because—

MARIE. Liliom doesn't support you, and he beats you—he thinks he can do whatever he likes just because he's Liliom. He's a bad one.

JULIE. He's not really bad.

MARIE. That night you sat on the bench together—he was gentle then.

JULIE. Yes, he was gentle.

MARIE. And afterwards he got wild again.

JULIE. Afterwards he got wild—sometimes. But that night on the bench—he was gentle. He's gentle now, sometimes, very gentle. After supper, when he stands there and listens to the music of the carousel, something comes over him—and he is gentle.

MARIE. Does he say anything?

JULIE. He doesn't say anything. He gets thoughtful and very quiet, and his big eyes stare straight ahead of him.

MARIE. Into your eyes?

JULIE. Not exactly. He's unhappy because he isn't working. That's really why he hit me on Monday.

MARIE. That's a fine reason for hitting you! Beats his wife because he isn't working, the ruffian!

JULIE. It preys on his mind—

MARIE. Did he hurt you?

JULIE. [*Very eagerly.*] Oh, no.

MRS. MUSKAT. [*Enters Center from Left, loudly dressed.*] Good morning. Is Liliom home?

JULIE. No.

MRS. MUSKAT. Gone out?

JULIE. He hasn't come home yet.

MRS. MUSKAT. I'll wait for him. [*She sits in chair down Left.*]

MARIE. [*Rising.*] You've got a lot of gall—to come here.

MRS. MUSKAT. Are you the lady of the house, my dear? Better look out or you'll get a slap in the mouth.

MARIE. How dare you set foot in Julie's house?

MRS. MUSKAT. [*To* JULIE.] Pay no attention to her, my child. You know what brings me here. That vagabond, that good-for-nothing, I've come to give him his bread and butter back.

MARIE. He's not dependent on you for his bread.

MRS. MUSKAT. [*To* JULIE.] Just ignore her, my child. She's just ignorant.

MARIE. [*Going on up Center.*] Good-bye.

JULIE. Good-bye.

MARIE. [*In the Center doorway, calling back.*] Sixty-six.

JULIE. Yes, sixty-six.

MARIE. Good-bye. [*She exits Center to Left.*]

[JULIE *starts toward door down Right.*]

MRS. MUSKAT. I paid him a krone a day, and on Sunday a gulden. And he got all the beer and cigars he wanted from the customers. [JULIE *pauses on the threshold, but does not answer.*] And he'd rather starve than beg my pardon. Well, I don't insist on that. I'll take him back without it. [JULIE *does not answer.*] The fact is the people ask for him—and, you see, I've got to consider business first. It's nothing to me if he starves. I wouldn't be here at all, if it wasn't for business—

[*She pauses, for* LILIOM *and* FICSUR *have entered Center from Left.* LILIOM *spits at* MRS. MUSKAT; *crosses Left and hangs up his hat and coat.*]

JULIE. Mrs. Muskat is here.

LILIOM. I see she is.

JULIE. You might say good morning.

LILIOM. [*Crossing to Center.*] What for? And what do *you* want, anyhow?

JULIE. I don't want anything.

LILIOM. Then keep your mouth shut. [*Pacing up and down.*] Next thing you'll be starting to nag again about my being out all night and out of work and living on your relations—

JULIE. I'm not saying anything.

LILIOM. But it's all on the tip of your tongue—I know you— [*Crosses down Right.*] Now don't start or you'll get another. [*He paces angrily up to couch and sits.*]

[*They are ALL a bit afraid of him, and shrink and look*

away as he passes them. FICSUR *shambles Left Center from place to place, his eyes cast down as if he were searching for something on the floor.*]

MRS. MUSKAT. [*Suddenly, to* FICSUR.] You're always dragging him out to play cards and drink with you. I'll have you locked up, I will.

FICSUR. I don't want to talk to you. You're too common. [*He goes out Center at back and lingers there in plain view.*]

[*There is a pause.*]

JULIE. Mrs. Muskat is here.

LILIOM. Well, why doesn't she open her mouth, if she has anything to say?

MRS. MUSKAT. [*Rises.*] Why do you go around with this man Ficsur? He'll get you mixed up in one of his robberies first thing you know.

LILIOM. [*Crossing down Center to Left.*] What's it to you who I go with? I do what I please. What do you want?

MRS. MUSKAT. You know what I want. [*Crosses to Center.*]

LILIOM. No, I don't. [*Sits down Left.*]

MRS. MUSKAT. What do you suppose I want? Think I've come just to pay a social call?

LILIOM. Do I owe you anything?

MRS. MUSKAT. Yes, you do—[LILIOM *rises as if to strike her*] but that's not what I came for. You're a fine one to come to for money! You earn so much these days! You know very well what I'm here for.

LILIOM. You've got Hollinger at the carousel, haven't you?

MRS. MUSKAT. Sure I have.

LILIOM. Well, what else do you want. He's as good as I am.

MRS. MUSKAT. You're quite right, my boy. He's every bit as good as you are. I'd not dream of letting him go. But one isn't enough any more. There's work enough for two—

LILIOM. One was enough when *I* was there.

MRS. MUSKAT. Well, I might let Hollinger go—

LILIOM. Why let him go, if he's so good?

MRS. MUSKAT. [*Shrugs her shoulders.*] Yes, he's good.

LILIOM. [*Crosses to* JULIE *Right.*] Ask your aunt if I can have a cup of coffee. [JULIE *exits up Right.*] So Hollinger is good, is he? [*Sits on Left end of table.*]

MRS. MUSKAT. [*Crossing to him.*] Why don't you stay home and sleep at night? You're a sight to look at.

LILIOM. He's good, is he?

MRS. MUSKAT. [*Brushes his hair with her hand.*] Push your hair back from your forehead.

LILIOM. [*Slaps her hand.*] Let my hair be. It's nothing to you.

MRS. MUSKAT. All right. But if I'd told you to let it

hang down over your eyes you'd have pushed it back—
I hear you've been beating her, this—this—

LILIOM. None of your business.

MRS. MUSKAT. You're a fine fellow! Beating a skinny
little thing like that! If you're tired of her, leave her,
but there's no use beating the poor—

LILIOM. Leave her, eh? You'd like that, wouldn't you?

MRS. MUSKAT. Don't flatter yourself. [*Quite embarrassed.*] Serves me right, too. If I had any sense I
wouldn't have run after you— My God, the things one
must do for the sake of business! If I could only sell
the carousel I wouldn't be sitting here. Come, Liliom,
if you have any sense, you'll come back. I'll pay you
well.

LILIOM. The carousel is crowded just the same *without
me?*

MRS. MUSKAT. Crowded, yes—but it's not the same.

LILIOM. Then you admit that you *do* miss me.

MRS. MUSKAT. Miss you? Not I. But the silly girls miss
you. They're always asking for you. Well, are you going to be sensible and some back?

LILIOM. And leave—her?

MRS. MUSKAT. You beat her, don't you?

LILIOM. No, I don't beat her. What's all this damn fool
talk about beating her? I hit her once—that was all—
and now the whole city seems to be talking about it.
You don't call that beating her, do you?

MRS. MUSKAT. All right, all right. I take it back. I don't want to get mixed up in it.

LILIOM. Beating her! As if I'd beat her—

MRS. MUSKAT. I can't make out why you're so concerned about her. You've been married to her two months—it's plain to see that you're sick of it—and out there is the carousel—and the show booths—and money —and you'd throw it all away. For what? Heavens, how can anyone be such a fool? [*Looks at him appraisingly.*] Where have you been all night? You look awful.

LILIOM. It's no business of yours.

MRS. MUSKAT. You never used to look like that. This life is telling on you. [*Pauses.*] Do you know—I've got a new organ.

LILIOM. [*Softly.*] I know.

MRS. MUSKAT. How did you know?

LILIOM. You can hear it—from here.

MRS. MUSKAT. It's a good one, eh?

LILIOM. [*Wistfully.*] Very good. Fine. It roars and snorts—so fine.

MRS. MUSKAT. You should hear it close by—it's heavenly. Even the carousel seems to know—it goes quicker. I got rid of those two horses—you know, the ones with the broken ears?

LILIOM. What have you put in their place?

MRS. MUSKAT. Guess.

LILIOM. Zebras?

MRS. MUSKAT. No—an automobile.

LILIOM. [*Transported.*] An automobile—

MRS. MUSKAT. Yes. If you've got any sense you'll come back. What good are you doing here? Out there is your *art,* the only thing you're fit for. You are an artist, not a respectable married man.

LILIOM. *Leave* her—this little—

MRS. MUSKAT. She'll be better off. She'll go back and be a servant girl again. As for you—you're an artist and you belong among artists. All the beer you want, cigars, a krone a day and a gulden on Sunday, and the girls, Liliom, the girls— I've always treated you right, haven't I? I bought you a watch, and—

LILIOM. She's not that kind. She'd never be a servant girl again.

MRS. MUSKAT. I suppose you think she'd kill herself. Don't worry. Heavens, if every girl was to commit suicide just because her— [*Finishes with a gesture.*]

LILIOM. [*Stares at her a moment, considering, then with sudden, smiling animation.*] So the people don't like Hollinger?

MRS. MUSKAT. You know very well they don't, you rascal.

LILIOM. Well—

MRS. MUSKAT. You've always been happy at the carousel. It's a great life—pretty girls and beer and cigars and music—a great life and an easy one. I'll tell you

what—come back and I'll give you a ring that used to
belong to my dear departed husband. Well, will you
come?

LILIOM. She's not that kind. She'd never be a servant
girl again. But—but—for my part—if I decide—that
needn't make any difference. I can go on living with her
even if I do go back to my art—

MRS. MUSKAT. My God!

LILIOM. What's the matter?

MRS. MUSKAT. Who ever heard of a married man— I
suppose you think all girls would be pleased to know
that you were running home to your wife every night.
It's ridiculous! When the people found out they'd laugh
themselves sick—

LILIOM. I know what you want.

MRS. MUSKAT. [*Refuses to meet his gaze.*] You flatter
yourself.

LILIOM. You'll give me that ring, too?

MRS. MUSKAT. [*Stroking his hair.*] Yes.

LILIOM. I'm not happy in this house.

MRS. MUSKAT. [*Still stroking his hair.*] Nobody takes
care of you.

[*They are silent.* JULIE *enters up Right, carrying a cup
of coffee to the table.* MRS. MUSKAT *removes her hand
from* LILIOM'S *head. There is a pause.* MRS. MUSKAT
strolls over Left and sits.]

LILIOM. Do you want anything?

JULIE. No. [*There is a pause. She exits slowly up Right.*]

MRS. MUSKAT. The old woman says there is a carpenter, a widower, who—

LILIOM. I know—I know—

JULIE. [*Reëntering crossing down Center.*] Liliom, before I forget, I have something to tell you.

LILIOM. All right.

JULIE. I've been wanting to tell you—in fact, I was going to tell you yesterday—

LILIOM. Go ahead.

JULIE. But I must tell you alone—if you'll come in—it will only take a minute.

LILIOM. Don't you see I'm busy now? Here I am talking business and you interrupt with—

JULIE. It'll only take a minute.

LILIOM. Get out of here, or—

JULIE. But I tell you it will only take a minute—

LILIOM. Will you get out of here?

JULIE. [*Courageously.*] No.

LILIOM. [*Rising.*] What's that! [*Draws back as though to hit her.*]

JULIE. No.

MRS. MUSKAT. [*Rises, too.*] Now don't start fighting. I'll go out and look at the photographs in the show-case a while and come back later for your answer. [*She exits Center to Left.*]

JULIE. You can hit me again if you like—don't look at me like that. I'm not afraid of you. I'm not afraid of anyone. I told you I had something to tell you.

LILIOM. Well, out with it—quick.

JULIE. I can't tell you so quick. Why don't you drink your coffee?

LILIOM. Is that what you wanted to tell me?

JULIE. No. By the time you've drunk your coffee I'll have told you.

LILIOM. [*Sits Left of table. Gets the coffee and sips it.*] Well?

JULIE. Yesterday my head ached—and you asked me—

LILIOM. Yes—

JULIE. Well—you see—that's what it is—

LILIOM. Are you sick?

JULIE. No.—But you wanted to know what my head-aches came from—and you said I seemed—changed.

LILIOM. Did I? I guess I meant the carpenter.

JULIE. I've been—what? The carpenter? No. It's something entirely different—it's awful hard to tell—but you'll have to know sooner or later—I'm not a bit —scared—because it's a perfectly natural thing—

LILIOM. [*Puts the coffee cup on the table.*] What?

JULIE. When—when a man and woman—live to-gether—

LILIOM. Yes.

JULIE. I'm going to have a baby. [*She exits swiftly up Right.*]

[*There is a pause.* FICSUR *appears at the hole back and looks in.*]

LILIOM. Ficsur! [FICSUR *sticks his head in Center door.*] Say, Ficsur,—Julie is going to have a baby.

FICSUR. Yes? What of it?

LILIOM. Nothing. [*Suddenly.*] Get out of here. [*Shoves him out. Center to Right.* LILIOM *comes down to Left of table; sits; takes up coffee cup.*]

MRS. MUSKAT. [*Reappears Center from Left.*] Has she gone?

LILIOM. [*Mumbles.*] Yes. [*Puts cup down.*]

MRS. MUSKAT. [*To above table.*] I might as well give you ten kronen in advance. [*Opens her purse.* LILIOM *takes up his cup.*] Here you are. [*She proffers some coins.* LILIOM *ignores her, swishes coffee around in the cup.*] Why don't you take it? [*Puts money on table.*]

LILIOM. [*Very nonchalantly, puts money nearer her on table; his cup poised ready to drink*] Go home, Mrs. Muskat.

MRS. MUSKAT. What's the matter with you?

LILIOM. [*Very grandly.*] Go home and let me finish my coffee in peace. Don't you see I'm at breakfast? [*Sips coffee, swishing it back and forth in his mouth.*]

MRS. MUSKAT. Have you gone crazy?

LILIOM. Will you get out of here? [*Turns to her threateningly.*]

MRS. MUSKAT. [*Restoring the coins to her purse.*] I'll never speak to you again as long as you live.

LILIOM. That worries me a lot.

MRS. MUSKAT. Good-bye!

LILIOM. Good-bye. [*As she exits Center to Left, he goes up to Center door and calls.*] Ficsur! [FICSUR *enters Center from Right. He pulls* FICSUR *in.*] Tell me, Ficsur. You said you knew a way to get a whole lot of money—

FICSUR. Sure I do.

LILIOM. How much?

FICSUR. More than you ever had in your life before. You leave it to an old hand like me.

MOTHER HOLLUNDER. [*Enters up Right. On hearing her* LILIOM *comes back to table and picks up cup.* FICSUR *to up Left Center.*] In the morning he must have his coffee, and at noon his soup, and in the evening coffee again—and plenty of firewood—and I'm expected to furnish it all. Give me back my cup and saucer.

[*The side shows of the amusement park have opened for business. The familiar NOISES begin to sound; clear above them all, but far in the distance, sounds the ORGAN of the carousel.*]

LILIOM. Now, Aunt Hollunder.

[*From now until the fall of the curtain it is apparent that the sound of the organ makes him more and more uneasy.*]

MOTHER HOLLUNDER. [*Up Center, to* FICSUR.] And

you, you vagabond, get out of here this minute or I'll call my son—

FICSUR. I have nothing to do with the likes of him. He's too common. [*But he slinks out Center to Right.*]

[MRS. HOLLUNDER *starts out up Right.*]

LILIOM. [*Crossing to Center.*] Aunt Hollunder!

MOTHER HOLLUNDER. [*Up Right Center.*] What now?

LILIOM. When your son was born—when you brought him into the world—

MOTHER HOLLUNDER. Well?

LILIOM. Nothing.

MOTHER HOLLUNDER. [*Muttering as she crosses down Right.*] Sleep it off, you good-for-nothing lout. Drink and play cards all night long—that's all you know how to do—and take the bread out of poor people's mouths— you can do that, too. [*She exits down Right.*]

LILIOM. Ficsur!

FICSUR. [*Appears at the hole.*] Julie's going to have a baby. You told me before.

[*WARN CURTAIN*]

LILIOM. This scheme—about the cashier of the leather factory—there's money in it—

FICSUR. Lots of money—but—it takes two to pull it off.

LILIOM. [*Meditatively.*] Yes. [*Uneasily.*] All right, Ficsur. Go away—and come back later.

[FICSUR *vanishes to Right. The ORGAN in the distant carousel drones incessantly.*]

LILIOM. [*Listens a while, then goes to the door down Right and calls.*] Aunt Hollunder! [*With naïve joy.*] Julie's going to have a baby. [*Then he goes to the hole in fence, jumps on the couch, looks out. Suddenly, in a voice that overtops the droning of the organ, he shouts as if addressing the far-off carousel.*] I'm going to be a father.

JULIE. [*Enters up Right.*] Liliom! What's the matter? What's happened?

LILIOM. [*Coming down from the couch.*] Nothing. [*Throws himself on the couch, buries his face in the cushion.*]

[JULIE *watches him a moment, comes over to him and covers him with a shawl. Then she goes on tip-toe to the door Center and remains standing in the doorway, looking out and listening to the droning of the organ.*]

THE CURTAIN FALLS

SCENE THREE

SCENE: *The setting is the same, later that afternoon.* LILIOM *is sitting at the table opposite* FICSUR, *who is teaching him a song.* JULIE *hovers in the background, engaged in some household task.*

FICSUR. Listen now. Here's the third verse. [*Sings hoarsely.*]

    "Look out, look out, my pretty lad,
      The damn police are on your trail;
      The nicest girl you ever had
      Has now commenced to weep and wail:
      Look out here comes the damn police,
      The damn police,
      The damn police,
      Look out here comes the damn police,
      They'll get you every time."

LILIOM. [*Sings.*]

    "Look out, look out, my pretty lad,
      The damn police—"

FICSUR, LILIOM. [*Sing together.*]

    "Are on your trail
      The nicest girl you ever had
      Has now commenced to weep and wail."

LILIOM. [*Alone.*]

    "Look out here comes the damn police,
      The damn police,
      The damn police—"

[JULIE, *troubled and uneasy, looks from one to the other, then exits up Right.*]

FICSUR. [*When she has gone, leans over to* LILIOM *and speaks furtively.*] As you go down Franzen Street you come to the railroad embankment. Beyond that—all the way to the leather factory—there's not a thing in sight, not even a watchman's hut.

LILIOM. And does he always come that way?

FICSUR. Yes. Not along the embankment, but down below along the path across the fields. Since last year he's been going alone. Before that he always used to have someone with him.

LILIOM. Every Saturday?

FICSUR. Every Saturday.

LILIOM. And the money? Where does he keep it?

FICSUR. In a leather bag. The whole week's pay for the workmen at the factory.

LILIOM. Much?

FICSUR. Sixteen thousand kronen. Quite a haul, what?

LILIOM. What's his name?

FICSUR. Linzman. He's a Jew.

LILIOM. The cashier?

FICSUR. Yes—but when he gets a knife between his ribs —or if I smash his skull for him—he won't be a cashier any more.

LILIOM. Does he have to be killed?

FICSUR. No, he doesn't *have* to be. He can give up the money *without* being killed—but most of these cashiers are peculiar—they'd *rather* be killed.

[JULIE *reënters, pretends to get something on the other side of the stage, then exits up Right. During the ensuing dialogue she keeps coming in and out in the same way, showing plainly that she is suspicious and anxious. She attempts to overhear what they are saying and, in spite of their caution, does catch a word here and there, which adds to her disquiet.*]

FICSUR. [*Catching sight of her, abruptly changes the conversation.*] And the next verse is:
    "And when you're in the prison cell
    They'll feed you bread and water."

FICSUR, LILIOM. [*Sing together.*]
    "They'll make your little sweetheart tell
    Them all the things you brought her.
    Look out here comes the damn police,
    The damn police,
    The damn police.
    Look out here comes the damn police
    They'll get you every time."

LILIOM. [*Sings alone.*]
    "And when you're in the prison cell
    They'll feed you bread and water—"

[*Breaks off as* JULIE *exits up Right.*] And when it's done, do we start right off for America?

FICSUR. No.

LILIOM. What then?

FICSUR. We bury the money for six months. That's the usual time. And after the sixth month we dig it up again.

LILIOM. And then?

FICSUR. Then you go on living just as usual for six months more—you don't touch a heller of the money.

LILIOM. In six months the baby will be born.

FICSUR. Then we'll take the baby with us, too. [*Rises.*] Three months before the time you'll go to work so as to be able to say you saved up your wages to get to America.

LILIOM. Which of us goes up and talks to him?

FICSUR. One of us talks to him with his mouth and the other talks with his knife. Depends on which you'd rather do. [*Pause.* LILIOM *appears undecided.*] I'll tell you what —you talk to him with your mouth.

LILIOM. Do you hear that?

FICSUR. What?

LILIOM. Outside—like the rattle of swords. [FICSUR *listens. After a pause,* LILIOM *continues.*] What do I say to him?

FICSUR. You say good evening to him and : "Excuse me, sir ; can you tell me the time?"

LILIOM. And then what?

FICSUR. By that time I'll have stuck him—and then you take *your* knife—

[*He stops as a* POLICEMAN *enters at Center from Left.*]

POLICEMAN. Good-day!

FICSUR, LILIOM. [*In unison.*] Good-day!

FICSUR. [*Calling toward up Right.*] Hey, photographer, come out.—Here's a customer. [*There is a pause. The* POLICEMAN *waits.* FICSUR *sings softly.*]
> "And when you're in the prison cell
>   They'll feed you bread and water
>   They'll make your little sweetheart tell."

FICSUR, LILIOM. [*Sing together, low.*]
>   "Them all the things you brought her.
>   Look out here comes the—"

[*They hum the rest so as not to let the* POLICEMAN *hear the words "the damn police." As they sing,* MOTHER HOLLUNDER *and her son enter up Right.*]

POLICEMAN. Do you make cabinet photographs?

YOUNG HOLLUNDER. Certainly, sir. [*Points to a rack of photographs on the wall.*] Take your choice, sir. Would you like one full length?

POLICEMAN. Yes, full length.

[MOTHER HOLLUNDER *pushes out the camera while her son poses the* POLICEMAN *up Left before the screen, runs from him to the camera and back again, now altering the pose, now ducking under the black cloth and pushing the camera nearer. Meanwhile* MOTHER HOLLUNDER *has fetched a plate from the dark room, Left, and thrust it in the camera. While this is going on,* LILIOM *and* FICSUR, *their heads together, speak in very low tones.*]

LILIOM. Belong around here?

FICSUR. Not around here.

LILOM. Where, then?

FICSUR. Suburban. [*There is a pause.*]

LILIOM. [*Bursts out suddenly in a rather grotesquely childish and overstrained lament.*] O God, what a dirty life I'm leading—God, God!

FICSUR. [*Reassuring him benevolently.*] Over in America it will be better, all right.

LILIOM. What's over there?

FICSUR. [*Virtuously.*] Factories—industries—

YOUNG HOLLUNDER. [*To the* POLICEMAN.] Now, quite still, please. One, two, three. [*Deftly removes the cover of the lens and in a few seconds restores it.*] Thank you.

MOTHER HOLLUNDER. The picture will be ready in five minutes.

POLICEMAN. Good. I'll come back in five minutes. How much do I owe you?

YOUNG HOLLUNDER. [*With exaggerated deference.*] You don't need to pay in advance, Mr. Commissioner.

[*The* POLICEMAN *salutes condescendingly and exits Center to Left.* MOTHER HOLLUNDER *carries the plate into the dark room.* YOUNG HOLLUNDER, *after pushing the camera back in place, follows her.*]

MOTHER HOLLUNDER. [*Reëntering. Muttering angrily as she crosses Right and passes* FICSUR *and* LILIOM.] You hang around and dirty the whole place up! Why don't you go take a walk? Things are going so well with you that you have to sing, eh? [*Confronting* FICSUR *sud-*

denly.] Weren't you frightened sick when you saw the policeman?

FICSUR. [*With loathing.*] Go 'way, or I'll step on you.

[*She exits down Right.*]

LILIOM. They like Hollinger at the carousel?

FICSUR. I should say they do.

LILIOM. Did you see the Muskat woman, too?

FICSUR. Sure. She takes care of Hollinger's hair.

LILIOM. Combs his hair?

FICSUR. She fixes him all up.

LILIOM. Let her fix him all she likes.

FICSUR. [*Urging him toward the up Right door.*] Go on. Now's your chance.

LILIOM. What for?

FICSUR. To get the knife.

LILIOM. What knife?

FICSUR. The kitchen knife. I've got a pocket-knife, but if he shows fight, we'll let him have the big knife.

LILIOM. What for? If he gets ugly, I'll bat him one over the head that'll make him squint for the rest of his life.

FICSUR. You've got to have something on you. You can't slit his throat with a bat over the head.

LILIOM. Must his throat be slit?

FICSUR. No, it *mustn't*. But if he asks for it. [*There is a pause.*] You'd like to sail on the big steamer, wouldn't you? And you want to see the factories over there, don't you? But you're not willing to inconvenience yourself a little for them.

LILIOM. If I take the knife, Julie will see me.

FICSUR. Take it so she won't see you.

LILIOM. [*Advances a few paces up Right toward the kitchen.* POLICEMAN *enters at back.* LILIOM *crosses down Right, knocks on the door.*] Here's the policeman!

MOTHER HOLLUNDER. [*Coming out down Right.*] One minute more, please. Just a minute. [*She exits to the dark room.*]

[LILIOM *hesitates a moment, then exits up Right. The* POLICEMAN *scrutinizes* FICSUR *mockingly.*]

FICSUR. [*Returns his stare, walks a few paces toward him, then deliberately turns his back. Suddenly he wheels around, points at the* POLICEMAN *and addresses him in a teasing, childish tone.*] Christiana Street at the corner of Retti!

POLICEMAN. [*Amazed, self-conscious.*] How do you know that?

FICSUR. I used to practice my profession in that neighborhood.

POLICEMAN. What is your profession?

FICSUR. Professor of pianola— [*The* POLICEMAN *glares, aware that the man is joking with him, twirls his moustache indignantly.*]

[YOUNG HOLLUNDER *comes out of the dark room and*

gives him the finished pictures. MOTHER HOLLUNDER
enters and exits up Right.]

YOUNG HOLLUNDER. Here you are, sir.

[*The* POLICEMAN *examines the photographs, pays for
them, starts to go, stops, glares at* FICSUR *and exits Center to Left. When he is gone,* FICSUR *goes to the Center
door and looks out after him.* YOUNG HOLLUNDER *exits
to dark room.* LILIOM *reënters, buttoning his coat.*]

FICSUR. [*Turns, sees* LILIOM.] What are you staring at?

LILIOM. I'm not staring. [*Jumps; startled, crosses Left
Center.*]

FICSUR. What then are you doing?

LILIOM. I'm thinking it over.

FICSUR. [*Comes very close him.*] Tell me then—what
will you say to him?

LILIOM. [*Unsteadily.*] I'll say—"Good evening— Excuse me, sir— Can you tell me the time?" And suppose
he answers me, what do I say to him?

FICSUR. He *won't* answer you.

LILIOM. Don't you think so?

FICSUR. No. [*Feeling for the knife under* LILIOM's *coat.*]
Where is it? Where did you put it?

LILIOM. [*Stonily motions with head.*] Left side.

FICSUR. That's right—over your heart. [*Feels it.*] Ah—
there it is—there—there's the blade—quite a big fellow,
isn't it—ah, here it begins to get narrower. [*Reaches the
tip of the knife.*] And here is its eye—that's what it sees

with. [JULIE *enters up Right, passes them slowly, watching them in silent terror, then stops.* FICSUR *nudges* LILIOM.] Sing, come on, sing!

LILIOM. [*In a quavering voice.*] "Look out for the damn police."

FICSUR. [*Joining, cheerily, loudly, marking time with the swaying of his body.*] "Look out, look out, my pretty lad."

LILIOM. "—look out, my pretty lad." [JULIE *goes out Center to Right.* LILIOM'S *glance follows her. When she has gone, he turns to* FICSUR.] At night—in my dreams —if his ghost comes back—what will I do then?

FICSUR. His ghost won't never come back.

LILIOM. Why not?

FICSUR. A Jew's ghost don't come back.

LILIOM. Well then—afterwards—

FICSUR. [*Impatiently.*] What do you mean—afterwards?

LILIOM. In the next world—when I come up before the Lord God—what'll I say then?

FICSUR. The likes of you will never come up before Him.

LILIOM. Why not?

FICSUR. Have you ever come up before the high court?

LILIOM. No.

FICSUR. Our kind comes up before the police magistrate —and the highest *we ever* get is the criminal court.

LILIOM. Will it be the same in the next world?

FICSUR. Just the same. We'll come up before a police magistrate, same as we did in this world.

LILIOM. A police magistrate?

FICSUR. Sure. For the rich folks—the Heavenly Court. For us poor people—only a police magistrate. For the rich folks—fine music and angels. For us—

LILIOM. For us?

FICSUR. For us, my son, there's only *justice*. In the next world there'll be lots of justice, yes, nothing but justice. And where there's justice there must be police magistrates; and where there're police magistrates, people like us get—

LILIOM. [*Interrupting.*] Good evening. Excuse me, sir, can you tell me the time? [*Lays his hand over his heart.*]

FICSUR. What do you put your hand there for?

LILIOM. My heart is jumping—under the knife.

FICSUR. Put it on the other side then. [*Looks out at the sky.*] It's time we started—we'll walk slow—

LILIOM. It's too early.

FICSUR. Come on.

[*They start up Center. As they are about to go,* JULIE *appears in the Center doorway, obstructing the way.*]

JULIE. Where are you going with him?

LILIOM. Where am I going with him?

JULIE. Stay home.

LILIOM. No.

JULIE. Stay home. It's going to rain soon, and you'll get wet.

FICSUR. [*Left of* LILIOM.] It won't rain.

JULIE. How do you know?

FICSUR. I always get notice in advance.

JULIE. Stay home. This evening the carpenter's coming. I've asked him to give you work.

LILIOM. I'm not a carpenter.

JULIE. [*More and more anxious, though she tries to conceal it.*] Stay home. Marie's coming with her intended to have their picture taken. She wants to introduce us to her intended husband.

LILIOM. I've seen enough intended husbands—

JULIE. Stay home. Marie's bringing some money, and I'll give it all to you.

LILIOM. [*Approaching the door.*] I'm going—for a walk —with Ficsur. We'll be right back.

JULIE. [*Forcing a smile to keep back her tears.*] If you stay home, I'll get you a glass of beer—or wine, if you prefer.

FICSUR. Coming or not?

JULIE. I'm not angry with you any more for hitting me.

LILIOM. [*Gruffly, but his gruffness is simulated to hide the fact that he cannot bear the sight of her suffering.*]

Stand out of the way—or I'll— [*He clenches his fist, she grasps his coat.*] Let me out!

JULIE. [*Trembling.*] What have you got under your coat?

LILIOM. [*Produces from his pocket a greasy pack of cards.*] Cards.

JULIE. [*Trembling, speaks very low.*] What's under your coat?

LILIOM. Let me out!

JULIE. [*Obstructing the way. Speaks quickly, eagerly, in a last effort to detain him.*] Marie's intended knows about a place for a married couple without children to be caretakers of a house on Arader Street. Rent free, a kitchen of your own, and the privilege of keeping chickens—

LILIOM. Get out of the way!

[JULIE *stands aside.* LILIOM *exits Center to Left.* FICSUR *follows him.* JULIE *remains standing meditatively in the Center doorway.*]

MOTHER HOLLUNDER. [*Pause. Entering up Right.*] I can't find my kitchen knife anywhere. Have you seen anything of it?

JULIE. [*Horrified.*] No.

MOTHER HOLLUNDER. It was on the kitchen table just a few minutes ago. No one was in there except Liliom.

JULIE. [*Down to her.*] He didn't take it.

MOTHER HOLLUNDER. No one else was in there.

JULIE. What would Liliom want with a kitchen knife?

MOTHER HOLLUNDER. He'd sell it and spend the money on drink.

JULIE. It just so happens—see how unjust you are to him —it just so happens that I went through all of Liliom's pockets just now—I wanted to see if he had any money on him. But he had nothing but a pack of cards.

MOTHER HOLLUNDER. [*Turns up Right, grumbling.*] Cards in his pocket—cards! The fine gentlemen have evidently gone off to their club to play a little game. [*She exits up Right.*]

[*After a pause* MARIE, *happy and beaming, appears Center from Left, and enters, followed by* WOLF.]

MARIE. Here we are! [*She takes* WOLF *by the hand and leads him, grinning shyly, to* JULIE, *who has turned at her call.*] Hello!

JULIE. [*Right of* WOLF.] Hello.

MARIE. [*Left of* WOLF.] Well, we're here.

JULIE. Yes.

WOLF. [*Bows awkwardly and extends his hand.*] My name is Wolf Beifeld.

JULIE. My name is Julie Zeller.

[*They shake hands. There is an embarrassed silence. Then, to relieve the situation,* WOLF *takes* JULIE'S *hand again and shakes it vigorously.*]

MARIE. Well—this is Wolf.

WOLF. Yes.

JULIE. Yes.

[*Another awkward silence.*]

MARIE. Where is Liliom?

WOLF. Yes, where is your husband?

JULIE. He's out.

MARIE. Where?

JULIE. Just for a walk.

MARIE. Is he?

JULIE. Yes.

WOLF. Oh!

[*Another silence.*]

MARIE. Wolf's got a new place. After the first of the month he won't have to stand outside any more. He's going to work in a club after the first of the month.

WOLF. [*Apologetically.*] She don't know yet how to explain these things just right—hehehe— Beginning the first I'm to be second steward at the Burger Club—a good job, if one conducts oneself properly.

JULIE. Yes?

WOLF. The pay—is quite good—but the main thing is the tips. When they play cards there's always a bit for the steward. The tips, I may say, amount to twenty, even thirty kronen every night.

MARIE. Yes.

WOLF. We've rented two rooms for ourselves to start with—and if things go well—

MARIE. Then we'll buy a house in the country.

WOLF. If one only tends to business and keeps honest. Of course, in the country we'll miss the city life, but if the good Lord sends us children—it's much healthier for children in the country.

[*There is a brief pause.*]

MARIE. Wolf's nice looking, isn't he?

JULIE. Yes.

MARIE. And he's a good boy, Wolf.

JULIE. [*Crossing to* MARIE; *embracing her.*] Yes.

MARIE. The only thing is—he's a Jew.

JULIE. Oh, well, you can get used to that.

MARIE. Well, aren't you going to wish us luck?

JULIE. Of course I do.

MARIE. And aren't you going to kiss Wolf, too?

JULIE. Him, too. [*She embraces* WOLF, *remains quite still a moment, her head resting on his shoulder.*]

WOLF. Why are you crying, my dear Mrs.— [*He looks questioningly at* MARIE *over* JULIE'S *shoulder.*]

MARIE. Because she has such a good heart. [*She becomes sentimental, too.*]

WOLF. [*Touched.*] We thank you for your heartfelt sympathy— [*He cannot restrain his own tears.*]

[*There is a pause before* MOTHER HOLLUNDER *and her son enter.* YOUNG HOLLUNDER *immediately puts back-*

ground screen over Left and busies himself with the camera.]

MOTHER HOLLUNDER. Now if you don't mind, we'll do it right away, before it gets too dark. [*She leads* MARIE *and* WOLF *into position before the background screen. Here they immediately fall into an awkward pose, smiling mechanically.* JULIE *sits Left of table.*] Full length?

MARIE. Please. Both figures full length.

WARN CURTAIN

MOTHER HOLLUNDER. Bride and groom?

MARIE. Yes.

MOTHER HOLLUNDER, YOUNG HOLLUNDER. [*Speak in unison, in loud professionally-expressionless tones.*] The lady looks at the gentleman and the gentleman looks straight into the camera.

MOTHER HOLLUNDER. [*Poses first* MARIE, *then* WOLF. *Adjusting the tripod to the back of* WOLF's *head.*] Now, if you please.

YOUNG HOLLUNDER. [*Who has crept under the black cloth, calls in muffled tones.*] That's good—that's very good!

MARIE. [*Stonily rigid, but very happy, trying to speak without altering her expression.*] Julie, dear, do we look all right?

JULIE. Yes, dear.

YOUNG HOLLUNDER. Now, if you please, hold still. I'll count up to three, and then you must hold perfectly still.

[*Grasps the cover of the lens and calls threateningly.*]
One—two—three! [*He removes the cover; there is utter
silence. But as he speaks the word "one" there is heard,
very faintly in the distance, the REFRAIN of the
thieves' song which* FICSUR *and* LILIOM *have been sing-
ing. The REFRAIN continues until the fall of the curtain. As he speaks the word "three" everybody is perfectly rigid save* JULIE, *who lets her head sink slowly to
the table. The distant REFRAIN dies out.*]

THE CURTAIN FALLS

SCENE FOUR

SCENE: *In the fields on the outskirts of the city. At back a railroad embankment crosses the stage obliquely. At Left on the embankment stands a semaphore. At Right on the embankment is a bell tower. An iron ladder at Right leads up to the embankment.*

At the foot of the embankment to Left Center is a pile of used railroad ties. In the background, through the underpass back Center, a view of trees, fences and fields; still further back a factory building and a cluster of little dwellings.

It is six o'clock of the same afternoon. Dusk has begun to fall.

LILIOM *is discovered on the ladder looking after the train which has just passed.* FICSUR *is seated on the ties Left Center.*

LILIOM. Can you still hear it snort?

FICSUR. Listen!

[*They watch the vanishing train.*]

LILIOM. If you put your ear on the tracks you can hear it go all the way to Vienna.

FICSUR. Huh!

LILIOM. The one that just puffed past us—it goes all the way to Vienna.

FICSUR. No further?

LILIOM. Yes—further, too.

[*There is a pause.*]

FICSUR. It must be near six. [*As* LILIOM *comes down the ladder and starts up Center.*] Where are you going?

LILIOM. Don't be afraid. I'm not giving you the slip.

FICSUR. Why should you give me the slip? That cashier has sixteen thousand kronen on him. Just be patient till he comes, then you can talk to him, nice and polite.

LILIOM. I say, "Good evening—excuse me, sir; what time is it?"

FICSUR. Then he tells you what time it is.

LILIOM. Suppose he don't come?

FICSUR. Nonsense! He's got to come. He pays off the workmen every Saturday. And this is Saturday, ain't it? [LILIOM *has ascended to the top of the ladder and is gazing along the tracks.*] What are you looking at up there?

[*Change semaphore light to amber.*]

LILIOM. The tracks go on and on—there's no end to them.

FICSUR. What's that to stare about?

LILIOM. Nothing—only I always look after the train. When you stand down there at night it snorts past you, and spits down.

FICSUR. Spits?

LILIOM. Yes, the engine. It spits down. And then the whole train rattles past and away—and you stand there —spat on—but it draws your eyes along with it.

FICSUR. Draws your eyes along?

LILIOM. Yes—whether you want to or not, you've got to look after it—as long as the tiniest bit of it is in sight.

FICSUR. Swell people sit in it.

LILIOM. And read newspapers.

FICSUR. And smoke cigars.

LILIOM. And inhale the smoke.

[*There is a short silence.*]

FICSUR. Is he coming?

LILIOM. [*Looks Right.*] Not yet. [*Silence again. Semaphore light changes to green.* LILIOM *comes down, speaks low, confidentially.*] Do you hear the telegraph wires?

FICSUR. I hear them when the wind blows.

LILIOM. Even when the wind doesn't blow you can hear them humming, humming— People talk through them.

FICSUR. Who?

LILIOM. Jews.

FICSUR. No—they telegraph.

LILIOM. They talk through them and from some other place they get answered. And it all goes through the iron strings—that's why they hum like that—they hum-m—

FICSUR. What do they hum?

LILIOM. They hum! ninety-nine, ninety-nine. Just listen.

FICSUR. What for?

LILIOM. That sparrow's listening, too. He's cocked one eye and looks at me as if to say: "I'd like to know what they're talking about."

FICSUR. You're looking at a bird?

LILIOM. He's looking at me, too.

FICSUR. Listen, you're sick! There's something the matter with you. Do you know what it is? Money. That bird has no money, either; that's why he cocks his eye.

LILIOM. Maybe.

FICSUR. Whoever has money don't cock his eye.

LILIOM. What then does he do?

FICSUR. He does most anything he wants. But nobody works unless he has money. We'll soon have money ourselves.

LILIOM. [*After a pause; loudly.*] I say, "Good evening. Excuse me, sir, can you tell me what time it is?"

FICSUR. [*Startled.*] He's not coming yet. Got the cards?

[LILIOM *gives him the pack of cards.*] Got any money?

LILIOM. [*Takes some coins from his trousers pocket and counts.*] Eleven.

FICSUR. [*Sits astride Left on the pile of ties and looks off Left.*] All right—eleven.

LILIOM. [*Sitting astride Right on the ties facing him.*] Put it up.

FICSUR. [*Puts the money on the ties; rapidly shuffles the cards.*] We'll play twenty-one. I'll bank. [*He deals deftly.*]

ʟɪʟɪᴏᴍ. [*Looks at his card.*] Good. I'll bet the bank.

ꜰɪᴄꜱᴜʀ. Must have an ace! [*Deals him a second card.*]

ʟɪʟɪᴏᴍ. Another one. [*He gets another card.*] Another. [*Gets still another.*] Over! [*Throws down his cards. ꜰɪᴄꜱᴜʀ gathers in the money.*] Come on!

ꜰɪᴄꜱᴜʀ. Come on what? Got no more money, have you?

ʟɪʟɪᴏᴍ. No.

ꜰɪᴄꜱᴜʀ. Then the game's over—unless you want to—

ʟɪʟɪᴏᴍ. What?

ꜰɪᴄꜱᴜʀ. Play on credit.

ʟɪʟɪᴏᴍ. You'll trust me?

ꜰɪᴄꜱᴜʀ. No— [*As ʟɪʟɪᴏᴍ strikes at him.*] but—I'll deduct it.

ʟɪʟɪᴏᴍ. Deduct it from what?

ꜰɪᴄꜱᴜʀ. From your share of the money. If *you* win you deduct from my share.

ʟɪʟɪᴏᴍ. [*Looks over his shoulder to see if the cashier is coming; nervous and ashamed.*] All right. How much is bank?

ꜰɪᴄꜱᴜʀ. That cashier is bringing us sixteen thousand kronen. Eight thousand of that is mine. Well, then, the bank is eight thousand.

ʟɪʟɪᴏᴍ. Good.

ꜰɪᴄꜱᴜʀ. Whoever has the most luck will have the most money. [*He deals.*]

LILIOM. Six hundred kronen. [FICSUR *gives him another card.*] Enough.

FICSUR. [*Laying out his own cards.*] Twenty-one. [*He shuffles rapidly.*]

LILIOM. [*Moves excitedly nearer to* FICSUR.] Well, then, double or nothing.

FICSUR. [*Dealing.*] Double or nothing.

LILIOM. [*Gets a card.*] Enough.

FICSUR. [*Laying out his own cards.*] Twenty-one. [*Shuffles rapidly again.*]

LILIOM. [*In alarm.*] You're not—cheating?

FICSUR. Me? Do I look like a cheat? [*Deals the cards again.*]

LILIOM. [*Glances nervously over his shoulder.*] A thousand.

FICSUR. [*Nonchalantly.*] Kronen?

LILIOM. Kronen. [*He gets a card.*] Another one. [*Gets another card.*] Over again! [*Like an inexperienced gambler who is losing heavily,* LILIOM *is very nervous. He plays dazedly, wildly, irrationally. From now on it is apparent that his only thought is to win his money back.*]

FICSUR. That makes twelve hundred you owe.

LILIOM. Double or nothing. [*He gets a card. He is greatly excited.*] Another one. [*Gets another card.*] Another. [*Throws down three cards.*]

FICSUR. [*Bends over and adds up the sum on the ground.*]

Ten—fourteen—twenty-three— You owe two thousand, four hundred.

LILIOM. Now what?

FICSUR. [*Takes a card out of the deck and gives it to him.*] Here's the red ace. You can play double or nothing again.

LILIOM. [*Eagerly.*] Good. [*Gets another card.*] Enough.

FICSUR. [*Turns up his own cards.*] Nineteen.

LILIOM. You win again. [*Almost imploring.*] Give me an ace again. Give me the green one. [*Takes a card.*] Double or nothing.

FICSUR. Not any more.

LILIOM. Why not?

FICSUR. Because if you lose you won't be able to pay. Double would be nine thousand six hundred. And you've only got eight thousand altogether.

LILIOM. [*Greatly excited.*] That—that—I call that—a dirty trick!

FICSUR. Three thousand, two hundred. That's all you can put up.

LILIOM. [*Eagerly.*] All right, then—three thousand, two hundred. [FICSUR *deals him a card.*] Enough.

FICSUR. I've got an ace myself. Now we'll have to take our time and squeeze 'em. [LILIOM *pushes closer to him as he takes up his cards and slowly, intently unfolds them.*] Twenty-one. [*He quickly puts the cards in his pocket.*]

[There is a pause.]

LILIOM. Now—now—I'll tell you now—you're a crook,
a low-down— [*A man is heard whistling off Right.*
LILIOM *crosses Right.* FICSUR *stands Left. Now* LINZ-
MAN *enters at Right. He is a strong, robust, red-bearded
Jew about 40 years of age. At his side he carries a leather
bag slung by a strap from his shoulder.* FICSUR *coughs
warningly, moves Right, pauses just behind* LINZMAN
and follows him. LILIOM *stands bewildered. He finds
himself facing* LINZMAN. *Trembling in every limb.*]
Good evening. Excuse me, sir, can you tell me the time?

[FICSUR *springs silently at* LINZMAN, *the little knife in
his right hand. But* LINZMAN *catches* FICSUR'S *right hand
with his own left and forces* FICSUR *to his knees. Simultaneously* LINZMAN *thrusts his right hand into his coat
pocket and produces a revolver which he points at* LIL-
IOM'S *breast.* LILIOM *is standing two paces away from
the revolver. There is a long pause.*]

LINZMAN. [*In a low, even voice.*] It is twenty-five minutes past six. [*Pauses, looks ironically down at* FICSUR.]
It's lucky I grabbed the hand with the knife instead of
the other one. [*Pauses again, looks appraisingly from
one to the other.*] Two fine birds! [*To* FICSUR.] I should
live so—Rothschild has more luck than you. [*To* LILIOM
who moves up Right.] I'd advise you to keep nice and
quiet. If you make one move, you'll get two bullets in
you. Just look into the barrel. You'll see some little things
in there made of lead.

FICSUR. Let me go. I didn't do anything.

LINZMAN. [*Mockingly shakes the hand which still holds
the knife.*] And this? What do you call this? Oh, yes, I

know. You thought I had an apple in my pocket, and you wanted to peel it. That's it. Forgive me for my error. I beg your pardon, sir. [*Blows whistle.*]

LILIOM. [*Jumps.*] But I—I—

LINZMAN. Yes, my son, I know. It's so simple. You only asked what time it is. Well, it's twenty-five minutes after six.

FICSUR. Let us go, honorable sir. We didn't do anything to you.

LINZMAN. In the first place, my son, I'm not an honorable sir. In the second place, for the same money, you could have said Your Excellency. But in the third place you'll find it very hard to beg off by flattering me.

LILIOM. [*Crossing down Right Center.*] But I—*I* really didn't do anything to you.

LINZMAN. Look behind you, my boy. Don't be afraid. [LILIOM *runs up Center; starts through underpass.*] Look behind you, but don't run away or I'll have to shoot you down. [LILIOM *turns his head slowly around and looks off Right.*] Who's coming up there?

LILIOM. [*Looking at* LINZMAN.] Policemen.

LINZMAN. [*To* FICSUR.] You hold still, or— [*To* LILIOM *teasingly.*] How many policemen are there?

LILIOM. [*His eyes cast down.*] Two.

LINZMAN. And what are the policemen sitting on?

LILIOM. Horses.

LINZMAN. And which can run faster, a horse or a man?

LILIOM. A horse.

LINZMAN. There, you see. It would be hard to get away now. [*Laughs.*] I never saw such an unlucky pair of highway robbers. I can't imagine worse luck. Just today I had to put a pistol in my pocket. And even if I hadn't— old Linzman is a match for four like you. But even that isn't all. Did you happen to notice, you oxen, what direction I came from? From the factory, didn't I? When I *went* there I had a nice bit of money with me. Sixteen thousand crowns! But now—not a heller. [*Calls off Right.*] Hey, come quicker, will you? This fellow is pulling pretty strong. [FICSUR *frees himself with a mighty wrench and darts rapidly off Left. As* LINZMAN *aims his pistol at the vanishing* FICSUR, LILIOM *runs up the ladder to the embankment.* LINZMAN *hesitates, perceives that* LILIOM *is the better target, points the pistol at him.*] Stop, or I'll shoot! [*Calls off Right to the* POLICEMEN.] Why don't you come down off your horses? [*His pistol is leveled at* LILIOM, *who stands on the embankment, facing the audience. From the Right a* POLICEMAN *appears, revolver in hand.*]

FIRST POLICEMAN. Stop!

LINZMAN. Well, my boy, do you still want to know what time it is? From ten to twelve years in prison!

LILIOM. You won't get me! [LINZMAN *laughs derisively.* LILIOM'S *face is uplifted to the sky. He bursts into laughter, half defiant, half self-pitying, and takes the kitchen knife from under his coat.*] Julie— [*The ring of farewell is in the word. He turns sideways, thrusts the knife deep in his breast, sways, falls and rolls down the far side of the embankment.*]

[*There is a long pause.* POLICEMEN *cross up through underpass and exit Right. From Right back the* POLICEMEN *are heard.*]

LINZMAN. [*Up Center.*] What's the matter? Stabbed himself?

FIRST POLICEMAN. Yes—and he seems to have made a thorough job of it.

[*They drag* LILIOM *in up Center.*]

LINZMAN. [*Excitedly to the* SECOND POLICEMAN.] I'll go and telephone to the hospital. [*He runs off Center to Left.*]

SECOND POLICEMAN. [*Up Center calling after* LINZMAN.] Go to Eisler's grocery store and telephone to the factory from there. They've a doctor there, too. [*To the other* POLICEMAN.] I'm going to tie up the horses. [*Comes down and starts up Right.*]

[*There is a pause. The semaphore changes to red.*]

FIRST POLICEMAN. Hey, Stephan!

SECOND POLICEMAN. What?

WARN CURTAIN

FIRST POLICEMAN. Shall I pull the knife out of his chest?

SECOND POLICEMAN. Better not, or he may bleed to death.

[*There is a pause.*]

FIRST POLICEMAN. [*Sits on ties Left Center.*] Stephan! [*Slaps his face.*]

SECOND POLICEMAN. Yes.

FIRST POLICEMAN. Lot of mosquitoes around here.

SECOND POLICEMAN. Yes.

FIRST POLICEMAN. Got a cigar?

SECOND POLICEMAN. No.

[*There is a pause.*]

FIRST POLICEMAN. A lot of good the new pay schedule's done us—made things worse than they used to be—we *get* more but we *have* less than we ever had. If the Government could be made to realize that. It's a thankless job at best. You work hard year after year, you get gray in the service, and slowly you die—yes.

SECOND POLICEMAN. That's right.

FIRST POLICEMAN. Yes.

[*In the distance is heard the BELL of the ambulance.*]

THE CURTAIN FALLS

SCENE FIVE

SCENE: *The photographic studio a half hour later that same evening.*

MOTHER HOLLUNDER, *her son,* MARIE *and* WOLF *stand in a group back Right, their heads together.* JULIE *stands apart from them, a few paces to the Left.*

YOUNG HOLLUNDER. [*Who has just come in, tells his story excitedly.*] They're bringing him now. Two workmen from the factory are carrying him on a stretcher.

WOLF. Where is the doctor?

YOUNG HOLLUNDER. A policeman telephoned to headquarters. The police surgeon ought to be here any minute.

MARIE. Maybe they'll pull him through after all.

YOUNG HOLLUNDER. He stabbed himself too deep in his chest. But he's still breathing. He can still talk, too, but very faintly. At first he lay there unconscious, but when they put him on the stretcher he came to.

WOLF. That was from the shaking.

MARIE. We'd better make room.

[*They make room. Two* WORKMEN *carry in* LILIOM, *Center from Left, on a stretcher which has four legs and stands about as high as a bed. They put the stretcher at Center, so that the head is at Right and the foot at Left. Then they unobtrusively join the* VILLAGERS *who have gathered at the Center door. Later, they go out.* JULIE *standing at the Left of the stretcher, where, without moving, she can see* LILIOM'S *face. The* OTHERS *crowd emotionally together near the door. The* FIRST POLICE-MAN *enters to Left of* JULIE.]

FIRST POLICEMAN. Are you his wife?

JULIE. Yes.

FIRST POLICEMAN. The doctor at the factory who band-aged him up forbade us to take him to the hospital.— Dangerous to move him that far. What he needs now is rest. Just let him be until the police surgeon comes. [*To the* GROUP *near the door.*] He's not to be disturbed.

[*They make way for him. He exits Center to Left. There is a pause.*]

WOLF. [*Gently urging the* OTHERS *out.*] Please—it's best if we all get out of here now. We'll only be in the way.

[VILLAGERS *exit Center to Left.*]

MARIE. [*To* JULIE.] Julie, what do you think? [JULIE *looks at her without answering.*] Julie, can I do anything to help? [JULIE *does not answer.*] We'll be just outside on the bench if you want us.

[MOTHER HOLLUNDER *and her son have gone out when first requested. Now* MARIE *and* WOLF *exit Center, too.* JULIE *sits on the edge of the stretcher and looks at* LILIOM. *He stretches his hand out to her. She clasps it. It is not quite dark yet.* BOTH *of them can still be plainly seen.*]

LILIOM. [*Raises himself with difficulty; speaks lightly at first, but later soberly, defiantly.*] Little—Julie—there's something—I want to tell you—like when you go to a restaurant—and you've finished eating—and it's time—to pay—then you can have to count up everything—everything you owe—well—I beat you—not because I was mad at you—no—only because I can't bear to see anyone crying. You always cried—on my account—and, well, you see,—I never learned a trade—what kind of a caretaker would I make? But anyhow—I wasn't going back to the carousel to fool with the girls. No, I spit on them all—understand?

JULIE. Yes.

LILIOM. And—as for Hollinger—he's good enough—Mrs. Muskat can get along all right with him. The jokes he tells are mine—and the people laugh when he tells them—but I don't care.—I didn't give you anything—no home—not even the food you ate—but you don't understand.—It's true I'm not much good—but I couldn't be a caretaker—and so I thought maybe it would be better over there—in America—do you see?

JULIE. Yes.

LILIOM. I'm not asking—forgiveness—I don't do that—I don't. Tell the baby—if you like.

JULIE. Yes.

LILIOM. Tell the baby—I wasn't much good—but tell him—if you ever talk about me—tell him—I thought—perhaps—over in America—but that's no affair of yours. [*Pause.*] I'm not asking forgiveness. For my part the police can come now.—If it's a boy—if it's a girl.—Perhaps I'll see the Lord God today.—Do you think I'll see Him?

JULIE. Yes.

LILIOM. I'm not afraid—of the police Up There—if they'll only let me come up in front of the Lord God Himself—not like down here where an officer stops you at the door. If the carpenter asks you—yes—be his wife —marry him. And the child—tell him he's his father.— He'll believe you—won't he?

JULIE. Yes.

LILIOM. When I beat you—I was right.—You mustn't always think—you mustn't always be right.—Liliom can be right once, too.—It's all the same to me who was right.—It's so dumb. Nobody's right—but they all think they are right.—A lot they know!

JULIE. Yes.

LILIOM. Julie—come—hold my hand tight.

JULIE. I'm holding it tight—all the time.

LILIOM. Tighter, still tighter—I'm going— [*Pauses.*] Julie—

JULIE. Good-bye.

[LILIOM *sinks slowly back and dies.* JULIE *frees her hand.* THE DOCTOR *enters Center with the* FIRST POLICE-MAN.]

DOCTOR. [*Left of* JULIE.] Good evening. His wife?

JULIE. [*Rising.*] Yes, sir.

[*Behind the* DOCTOR *and* POLICEMAN *enter* MARIE, WOLF, MOTHER HOLLUNDER, YOUNG HOLLUNDER *and* MRS. MUSKAT. *They remain respectfully at the doorway.*]

DOCTOR. [*Bends over* LILIOM *and examines him.*] A light, if you please. [JULIE *fetches a burning candle from the dark room. The* DOCTOR *examines* LILIOM *briefly in the candle-light, then turns suddenly away.*] Have you pen and ink?

WOLF. [*Proffering a pen.*] A fountain-pen—American—

DOCTOR. [*Takes a printed form from his pocket; speaks as he writes out the death certificate as he stands.*] My poor woman, your husband is dead—there's nothing to be done for him—the good God will help him now— I'll leave this certificate with you. You will give it to the people from the hospital when they come— I'll arrange for the body to be removed at once. Please give me a towel and soap.

POLICEMAN. I've got them for you out here, sir. [*Points to door at back.*]

DOCTOR. God be with you, my good woman.

JULIE. [*Puts candle on the table.*] Thank you, sir.

[*The* DOCTOR *and* POLICEMAN *exit Center. The* OTHERS *slowly draw nearer.*]

MARIE. [*To Right of* JULIE *who is above table.*] Poor Julie. May he rest in peace, poor man, but as for you—please don't be angry with me for saying it—but you're better off this way.

MOTHER HOLLUNDER. He is better off, the poor fellow, and so are you.

MARIE. Much better, Julie—you are young—and one of these days some good man will come along. Am I right?

WOLF. She's right.

MARIE. Julie, tell me, am I right?

JULIE. You are right, dear; you are very good.

YOUNG HOLLUNDER. There's a good man—the carpenter. Oh, I can speak of it now. He comes here every day on some excuse or other—and he never fails to ask for you.

MARIE. A widower—with two children.

MOTHER HOLLUNDER. He's better off, poor fellow—and so are you. He was a bad man.

MARIE. He wasn't good-hearted. Was he, Wolf?

WOLF. No, I must say, he really wasn't. No. Liliom wasn't a good man. A good man doesn't strike a woman.

MARIE. Am I right? Tell me, Julie, am I right?

JULIE. You are right, dear.

YOUNG HOLLUNDER. It's really a good thing for her it happened.

MOTHER HOLLUNDER. He's better off—and so is she.

WOLF. Now you have your freedom again. How old are you?

JULIE. Eighteen.

WOLF. Eighteen. A mere child! Am I right?

JULIE. You are right, Wolf. You are kind.

YOUNG HOLLUNDER. Lucky for you it happened, isn't it?

JULIE. Yes.

YOUNG HOLLUNDER. All you had before was bad luck. If it weren't for my mother you wouldn't have had a roof over your head or a bite to eat—and now Autumn's coming and Winter. You couldn't have lived in this shack in the Winter time, could you?

MARIE. Certainly not! You'd have frozen like the birds in the fields. Am I right, Julie?

JULIE. Yes, Marie.

MARIE. A year from now you will have forgotten all about him, won't you?

JULIE. You are right, Marie.

WOLF. If you need anything, count on us. We'll go now. But tomorrow morning we'll be back. Come, Marie. God be with you. [*Offers* JULIE *his hand.*]

JULIE. God be with you.

MARIE. [*Embraces* JULIE, *weeping.*] It's the best thing that could have happened to you, Julie, the best thing.

JULIE. Don't cry, Marie.

[MARIE *and* WOLF *exit Center to Left.*]

MOTHER HOLLUNDER. I'll make a little black coffee. You haven't had a thing to eat today. Then you'll come home with us.

[*The* HOLLUNDERS *exit up Right.* MRS. MUSKAT *comes over to Right of* JULIE.]

MRS. MUSKAT. Would you mind if I—looked at him?

JULIE. He used to work for you.

MRS. MUSKAT. [*Contemplates the body; turns to* JULIE.] Won't you make up with me?

JULIE. I wasn't angry with you.

MRS. MUSKAT. But you were. Let's make it up.

JULIE. [*Raising her voice serenely, almost triumphantly.*] I've nothing to make up with *you.*

MRS. MUSKAT. But I have with you. Everyone says hard things against the poor dead boy—except us two. You don't say he was bad.

JULIE. [*Raising her voice yet higher, this time on a defiant, wholly triumphant note.*] Yes, I *do.*

MRS. MUSKAT. I understand, my child. But he beat me, too. What does that matter? I've forgotten it.

JULIE. [*From now on answers her coldly, dryly, without looking at her.*] That's your own affair.

MRS. MUSKAT. If I can help you in any way—

JULIE. There's nothing I need.

MRS. MUSKAT. I still owe him two kronen, back pay.

JULIE. You should have paid him.

MRS. MUSKAT. Now that the poor fellow is dead I thought perhaps it would be the same if I paid you.

JULIE. I've nothing to do with it.

MRS. MUSKAT. All right. Please don't think I'm trying to force myself on you. I stayed because we two are the only ones on earth who loved him. That's why I thought we ought to stick together.

JULIE. No, thank you.

MRS. MUSKAT. Then you couldn't have loved him as I did.

JULIE. No.

MRS. MUSKAT. I loved him better.

JULIE. Yes.

MRS. MUSKAT. Good-bye.

JULIE. Good-bye. [MRS. MUSKAT *exits Center to Left. JULIE goes up, then comes down and takes* LILIOM's *head in her hands.*] Sleep, Liliom, sleep—it's no business of hers—I never even told you—but now I'll tell you—now I'll tell you—you bad, quick-tempered, rough, unhappy, wicked—*dear* boy—sleep peacefully, Liliom—they can't understand how I feel—I can't even explain to you—not even to you—how I feel—you'd only laugh at me—but you can't hear me any more. [*Between tender motherliness and reproach, yet with great love in her voice.*] It was wicked of you to beat me—on the breast and on the head and face—but you're gone now.—You treated me badly—that was wicked of you—but sleep peacefully, Liliom—you bad, bad boy, you—I love you—I never told you before—I was ashamed—but now I've told you —I love you. Liliom—sleep—my boy—sleep. [*She rises, gets Bible on table, sits down near the candle and reads softly to herself, so that, not the words, but an inarticulate murmur is heard. Matthew 5–1. The* CARPENTER *enters Center from Left.* JULIE *murmurs.*] "And seeing the multitudes he went up into a mountain and when he was set his disciples came unto him and he opened his mouth and taught them saying: 'Blessed.' "

CARPENTER. [*Stands near the door; in the dimness of the place he can scarcely be seen.*] Miss Julie—

JULIE. [*Without alarm.*] Who is that?

CARPENTER. [*Very slowly.*] The carpenter.

JULIE. What does the carpenter want?

CARPENTER. Can I be of help to you in any way? Shall I stay here with you?

JULIE. [*Gratefully, but firmly.*] Don't stay, carpenter.

CARPENTER. Shall I come back tomorrow?

JULIE. Not tomorrow, either.

CARPENTER. Don't be offended, Miss Julie, but I'd like to know—you see, I'm not a young man any more—I have two children—and if I'm to come back any more—I'd like to know—if there's any use—

JULIE. No use, carpenter.

CARPENTER. [*As he exits Center to Left.*] God be with you.

[JULIE *resumes her reading.* FICSUR *enters up Right, slinks furtively sideways to the stretcher, looks at* LILIOM, *touches his face, draws back startled.* JULIE *looks up from her reading.* FICSUR *takes fright, slinks away from the stretcher, biting his nails.* JULIE *rises.* FICSUR *looks at her half fearfully. With her piercing glance upon him he slinks to the Center doorway, where he pauses and speaks.*]

FICSUR. The old woman asked me to tell you that coffee is ready, and you are to come in.

[JULIE *goes to the door up Right.* FICSUR *withdraws until she has closed the door behind her. Then he reappears in the doorway, stands on tiptoes, looks at* LILIOM, *then exits Left. Now the body lies alone. After a brief silence the Dead March is heard, distant at first, but gradually coming nearer. It is very much like the music of the carousel, but slower, graver, more exalted. The melody, too, is the same, yet the tempo is altered and contrapuntal measures of the thieves' song are intertwined in it.* TWO MEN *in black, with heavy sticks, soft black hats and black gloves, appear in the doorway at back and stride slowly into the room. Their faces are beardless, marble white, grave and benign. One stops in front of the stretcher, the other a pace to the Right. From above a dim violet light illuminates their faces. MUSIC stops.*]

THE FIRST. [*To* LILIOM.] Rise and come with us.

THE SECOND. [*Politely.*] You're under arrest.

THE FIRST. [*Somewhat louder, but always in a gentle, low, resonant voice.*] Do you hear? Rise. Don't you hear?

THE SECOND. We are the police.

THE FIRST. [*Bends down, touches* LILIOM'S *shoulder.*] Get up and come with us.

[LILIOM'S *hand drops down very, very slowly.*]

THE SECOND. Come along.

THE FIRST. [*Paternally.*] These people suppose that when they die all their difficulties are solved for them.

WARN CURTAIN

THE SECOND. [*Raising his voice sternly.*] That simply by thrusting a knife in your heart and making it stop beating you can leave your wife behind with a child in her womb—

THE FIRST. It is not as simple as that.

THE SECOND. Such things are not settled so easily.

THE FIRST. Come along. You will have to give an account of yourself. [*As both bow their heads, he continues softly.*] We are God's police. [*An expression of glad relief lights upon* LILIOM'S *face. He rises from the stretcher.*] Come.

THE SECOND. You mortals don't get off quite as easy as that.

THE FIRST. Come. [*Softly.*] The end is not as abrupt as that. Your name is still spoken. Your face is still remembered. And what you said, and what you did, and what you failed to do—these are still remembered. Remembered, too, are the manner of your glance, the ring of your voice, the clasp of your hand and how your step sounded—as long as one is left who remembers you, so long is the matter unended. Before the end there is much to be undone. Until you are quite forgotten, my son, you will not be finished with the earth—even though you *are* dead.

THE SECOND. [*Very gently.*] Come.

[*The Dead March begins again. All three exit at back,* LILIOM *in the Center; the* OTHERS *following slowly. The stage is empty and quite dark save for the candle which burns by the stretcher, on which, in the shadows, the covers are so arranged that one cannot*

*quite be sure that a body is not still lying on it. The
MUSIC dies out in the distance as if it had followed
LILIOM and the TWO POLICEMEN. The candle flickers and
goes out. There is a brief interval of silence and total
darkness before JULIE returns with lamp and crosses to
stretcher, makes a caressing movement over the couch,
where she presumably still sees the body. Goes back to
the table, picks up the Bible and begins to read.* "Blessed
are the pure in heart for they shall see God"—"For they
shall see God!"—

THE CURTAIN FALLS

SCENE SIX

SCENE: *In the Beyond. A whitewashed courtroom. There is grated iron door Right. The main entrance is Right Center at back and another door is down Left. There is a window Left Center at back through which can be seen a vista of rose-colored clouds. There is a bench Center; and at Left is a low platform with judge's bench.*

Two MEN *are on the Center bench when the Curtain rises. One is richly, the other poorly dressed.*

Passing the window at back as though coming up from below appear LILIOM *and the two* POLICEMEN. *The BELL rings.*

An old GUARD *enters at Left. He is bald and has a long white beard. He wears the conventional police uniform. He goes to the door Right Center, opens it, exchanges silent greetings with the two* POLICEMEN *who enter with* LILIOM, *and closes the door again.*

LILIOM *looks wonderingly around.*

FIRST POLICEMAN. [*To the old* GUARD.] Announce us.

[*The* GUARD *exits at Left.*]

LILIOM. Is this it?

SECOND POLICEMAN. Yes, my son.

LILIOM. This is the police court?

SECOND POLICEMAN. Yes, my son. The part for suicide cases.

LILIOM. And what happens here?

FIRST POLICEMAN. Here justice is done. Sit down.

[LILIOM *looks at bench where there is not enough room. Sits Left on bench next to the* TWO MEN *shoving them over. The* TWO POLICEMEN *stand silent up back of bench.*]

RICHLY DRESSED MAN. [*Whispers.*] Suicide, too?

LILIOM. Yes.

RICHLY DRESSED MAN. [*Points to the* POORLY DRESSED MAN.] So's he. [*Introducing himself.*] My name is Reich.

POORLY DRESSED MAN. [*Whispers, too.*] My name is Stephan Kadar.

[LILIOM *only looks at them.*]

POORLY DRESSED MAN. And you? What's your name?

LILIOM. None of your business.

[*Both move a bit away from him.*]

POORLY DRESSED MAN. I did it by jumping out of a window.

RICHLY DRESSED MAN. I did it with a pistol—and you?

LILIOM. With a knife.

[*They move a bit further away from him.*]

RICHLY DRESSED MAN. A pistol is cleaner.

LILIOM. If I had the price of a pistol—

SECOND POLICEMAN. Silence!

[*The* POLICE MAGISTRATE *enters Left. He has a long white beard, is bald, but only in profile can be seen on his head a single tuft of snow-white hair. The* GUARD *re-enters behind him and stands back of* MAGISTRATE. *As the* MAGISTRATE *enters,* ALL *rise, except* LILIOM, *who remains surlily seated. When the* MAGISTRATE *sits down, so do the* OTHERS.]

GUARD. Yesterday's cases, your honor. The numbers are entered in the docket.

MAGISTRATE. Number 16,472.

FIRST POLICEMAN. [*Looks in his notebook, beckons the* RICHLY DRESSED MAN.] Stand up, please.

[THE RICHLY DRESSED MAN *rises, crosses slowly to Left Center.*]

MAGISTRATE. Your name?

RICHLY DRESSED MAN. Doctor Reich.

MAGISTRATE. Age?

RICHLY DRESSED MAN. Forty-two, married, Jew.

MAGISTRATE. [*With a gesture of dismissal.*] Religion does not interest us here—why did you kill yourself?

RICHLY DRESSED MAN. On account of debts.

MAGISTRATE. What good did you do on earth?

RICHLY DRESSED MAN. I was a lawyer—

MAGISTRATE. [*Coughs significantly.*] Yes—we'll discuss that later. For the present I shall only ask you: Would you like to go back to earth once more before sunrise? I advise you that you have the right to go if you choose. Do you understand?

RICHLY DRESSED MAN. Yes, sir.

MAGISTRATE. He who takes his life is apt, in his haste and his excitement, to forget something. Is there anything important down there you have left undone? Something to tell someone? Something to undo?

RICHLY DRESSED MAN. My debts—

MAGISTRATE. They do not matter here. Here we are concerned only with the affairs of the soul.

RICHLY DRESSED MAN. Then—if you please—when I left —the house—my youngest son, Oscar—was asleep. I didn't trust myself to wake him—and bid him good-bye. I would have liked—to kiss him good-bye.

MAGISTRATE. [*To* SECOND POLICEMAN.] You will take Dr. Reich back and let him kiss his son Oscar.

SECOND POLICEMAN. Come with me, please.

RICHLY DRESSED MAN. [*To* THE MAGISTRATE.] I thank you. [*He bows and exits Right Center with* SECOND POLICEMAN.]

MAGISTRATE. [*After making an entry in the docket.*] Number 16,473.

FIRST POLICEMAN. [*Looks in his notebook, then beckons* LILIOM.] Stand up.

LILIOM. You said *please* to *him*. [*He rises, crosses to Left Center.*]

MAGISTRATE. Your name?

LILIOM. Liliom.

MAGISTRATE. Isn't that your nickname?

LILIOM. Yes.

MAGISTRATE. What is your right name?

LILIOM. Andreas.

MAGISTRATE. And your last name?

LILIOM. Zavoczki—after my mother.

MAGISTRATE. Your age?

LILIOM. Twenty-four.

MAGISTRATE. What good did *you* do on earth? [LILIOM *is silent.*] Why did you take your life? [LILIOM *does not answer. The* MAGISTRATE *addresses* FIRST POLICEMAN.] Take that knife away from him. [FIRST POLICEMAN *does so.*] It will be returned to you, if you go back to earth.

LILIOM. Do I go back to earth again?

MAGISTRATE. Just answer my questions.

LILIOM. I wasn't answering then, I was asking if—

MAGISTRATE. You don't ask questions here. You only answer. Only answer. Andreas Zavoczki! I ask you whether there is anything on earth you neglected to accomplish? Anything down there you would like to do?

LILIOM. Yes.

MAGISTRATE. What is it?

LILIOM. I'd like to break Ficsur's head for him.

MAGISTRATE. Punishment is our office. Is there nothing else on earth you'd like to do?

LILIOM. I don't know—I guess, as long as I'm here, I'll not go back.

MAGISTRATE. [*To* FIRST POLICEMAN.] Note that. He waives his right. [LILIOM *starts back to the bench.*] Stay where you are. You are aware that you left your wife without food or shelter?

LILIOM. Yes.

MAGISTRATE. Don't you regret it?

LILIOM. No.

MAGISTRATE. You are aware that your wife is pregnant, and that in six months a child will be born?

LILIOM. I know.

MAGISTRATE. And that the child, too, will be without food or shelter? Do you regret that?

LILIOM. As long as I won't be there, what's it got to do with me?

MAGISTRATE. Don't try to deceive us, Andreas Zavoczki. We see through you as through a pane of glass.

LILIOM. If you see so much, what do you want to ask me for? Why don't you let me rest—in peace?

MAGISTRATE. First you must earn your rest.

LILIOM. I want—only—to sleep.

MAGISTRATE. Your obstinacy won't help you. Here patience is endless as time. We can wait.

LILIOM. Can I ask something—I'd like to know—if Your Honor will tell me—whether the baby will be a boy or a girl.

MAGISTRATE. You shall see that for yourself.

LILIOM. [*Excitedly.*] I'll see the baby?

MAGISTRATE. When you do it won't be a baby any more. But we haven't reached that question yet.

LILIOM. I'll see it?

MAGISTRATE. Again I ask you: Do you not regret that you deserted your wife and child; that you were a bad husband, a bad father?

LILIOM. A bad husband?

MAGISTRATE. Yes.

LILIOM. And a bad father?

MAGISTRATE. That, too.

LILIOM. I couldn't get work—and I couldn't bear to see Julie—all the time—all the time—

MAGISTRATE. Weeping! Why are you ashamed to say it? You couldn't bear to see her weeping. Why are you afraid of that word? And why are you ashamed that you loved her?

LILIOM. [*Shrugs his shoulders.*] Who's ashamed? But I couldn't bear to see her—and that's why I was bad to her. You see, it wouldn't do to go back to the carousel— and Ficsur came along with his talk about—that other thing—and all of a sudden it happened, I don't know how. The police and the Jew with the pistol—and there I stood—and I'd lost the money playing cards—and I didn't want to be put in prison [*Demanding justification.*] Maybe I was wrong not to go out and steal when there was nothing to eat in the house? Should I have gone out to steal for Julie?

MAGISTRATE. [*Emphatically.*] Yes.

LILIOM. [*After an astounded pause. Points down.*] The police down *there* never said that.

MAGISTRATE. You beat that poor, frail girl; you beat her because she loved you. How could you do that?

LILIOM. We argued with each other—she said this and I said that—and because she was right I couldn't answer her—and I got mad—and the anger rose up in me—until it reached here [*points to his throat*] and then I beat her.

MAGISTRATE. Are you sorry?

LILIOM. [*Shakes his head, but cannot utter the word "no"; continues softly.*] When I touched her slender throat—then—if you like—you might say— [*Falters, looks embarrassed at the* MAGISTRATE.]

MAGISTRATE. [*Confidently expectant.*] Are you sorry?

LILIOM. [*With a stare.*] I'm not sorry for anything.

MAGISTRATE. Liliom, Liliom, it will be difficult to help you.

LILIOM. I'm not asking any help.

MAGISTRATE. You were offered employment as a caretaker on Arader Street. [*To the* GUARD.] Where is that entered?

THE GUARD. In the small docket. [*Hands him the open book.*]

MAGISTRATE. [*Looks in it.*] Rooms, kitchen, quarterly wages, the privilege of keeping poultry. Why didn't you accept it?

LILIOM. I'm not a caretaker. I'm no good at caretaking.
To be a caretaker—you have to *be* a caretaker—

MAGISTRATE. If I said to you now : Liliom, go back on
your stretcher. Tomorrow morning you will arise alive
and well again. Would you be a caretaker then?

LILIOM. No.

MAGISTRATE. Why not?

LILIOM. Because—because that's just why I died.

MAGISTRATE. That is not true, my son. You died because
you loved little Julie and the child she is bearing under
her heart.

LILIOM. No.

MAGISTRATE. Look me in the eye.

LILIOM. [*Looks him in the eye.*] No. [*Shifts his eye
when he says it.*]

MAGISTRATE. [*Stroking his beard.*] Liliom, Liliom, if it
were not for our Heavenly patience— Go back to your
seat. Number 16,474.

FIRST POLICEMAN. [*Looks in his notebook.*] Stephan
Kadar.

[THE POORLY DRESSED MAN *rises; crosses to Left Center.* LILIOM *sits on bench.*]

MAGISTRATE. You came out today?

POORLY DRESSED MAN. Today.

MAGISTRATE. [*Indicating the door at Right.*] How long
were you in there?

POORLY DRESSED MAN. Thirteen years.

MAGISTRATE. Officer, you went to earth with him?

FIRST POLICEMAN. Yes, sir.

MAGISTRATE. Stephan Kadar, after thirteen years of purification by fire you returned to earth to give proof that your soul had been burned clean. What good deed did you perform?

POORLY DRESSED MAN. When I came to the village and looked in the window of our cottage I saw my poor little orphans sleeping peacefully. But it was raining and the rain beat into the room through a hole in the roof. So I went and fixed the roof so it wouldn't rain in any more. My hammering woke them up and they were afraid. But their mother came in to them and comforted them. She said to them: "Don't cry! It's your poor, dear father hammering up there. He's come back from the other world to fix the roof for us."

MAGISTRATE. Officer?

FIRST POLICEMAN. That what happened.

MAGISTRATE. Stephan Kadar, you have done a good deed. What you did will be written in books to gladden the hearts of children who read them. [*Indicates the door at Left which the* GUARD *opens in a flood of white light.*] The door is open to you. The eternal light awaits you. [FIRST POLICEMAN *escorts the* POORLY DRESSED MAN *out at Left with great deference; then returns to up Right Center.*] Liliom! [LILIOM *rises.*] You have heard?

LILIOM. Yes.

MAGISTRATE. When this man first appeared before us

he was as stubborn as you. But now he has purified himself and withstood the test. He has done a good deed.

LILIOM. What's he done, anyhow? Any roofer can fix a roof. It's much harder to be a barker in an amusement park.

MAGISTRATE. Liliom, you shall remain for sixteen years in the crimson fire until your child is full grown. By that time your pride and your stubbornness will have been burnt out of you. And when your daughter—

LILIOM. My daughter!

MAGISTRATE. When your daughter has reached the age of sixteen— [LILIOM *bows his head, covers his eyes with his hands, and to keep from weeping laughs defiantly, sadly.*] When your daughter has reached the age of sixteen you will be sent for one day back to earth.

LILIOM. Me?

MAGISTRATE. Yes—just as you may have read in the legends of how the dead reappear on earth for a time.

LILIOM. I never believed them.

MAGISTRATE. Now you see they are true. You will go back to earth one day to show how far the purification of your soul has progressed.

LILIOM. Then I must show what I can do—like when you apply for a job—as a coachman?

WARN CURTAIN

MAGISTRATE. Yes—it is a test.

LILIOM. And will I be told what I have to do?

MAGISTRATE. No.

LILIOM. How will I know, then?

MAGISTRATE. You must decide that for yourself. That's what you burn sixteen years for. And if you do something good, something splendid for your child, then—

LILIOM. [*Laughs sadly.*] Then? [ALL *stand up and bow their heads reverently. There is a pause.*] Then?

MAGISTRATE. Now I'll bid you farewell, Liliom. Sixteen years and a day shall pass before I see you again. When you have returned from earth you will come up before me again. Take heed and think well of some good deed to do for your child. On that will depend which door shall be opened to you up here. Now go, Liliom. [*He exits Left.*]

[THE GUARD *stands at attention. There is a pause.*]

FIRST POLICEMAN. [*Approaches* LILIOM.] Come along, my son. [*He goes to the door Right; pulls open the bolt and waits.*]

LILIOM. [*To the* GUARD, *softly.*] Say, Officer.

THE GUARD. What do you want?

LILIOM. Please—can I get—have you got—?

THE GUARD. What?

LILIOM. [*Whispers.*] A cigarette?

[*The* GUARD *stares at him. Then his expression softens. He takes a cigarette from his pocket and, crossing to* LILIOM—*who has gone over to the door Right*—*gives him the cigarette.* FIRST POLICEMAN *throws open the door. An intense rose-colored light streams in. The glow of it is so strong that it blinds* LILIOM *and he takes a step backward and bows his head and covers his eyes with his hand before he steps forward into the light and exits.*]

THE CURTAIN FALLS

SCENE SEVEN

Sixteen years later.

SCENE: *There is a small, neat house with a porch and
tiny garden down Left. A low fence runs from Right
and slants down Left to lower edge of the house. There
is a gate in this slanted section. Below the fence is a
street. There is a shrine Center at back with a bench in
front of it. A table with chairs on the porch. Beyond
the fence is a view of a suburban street which blends
into a broad vista of tilled fields.*
It is a bright Sunday in Spring.
JULIE, *her daughter* LOUISE, WOLF *and* MARIE *are discovered.* WOLF, *prosperously dressed, is Right Center
outside gate.* MARIE *somewhat elaborate, with a huge
hat, is Right of gate.*

JULIE. [*Left of gate.*] You could stay for lunch.

MARIE. Impossible, dear. Since he became the proprietor
of the Café Sorrento, Wolf simply *has* to be there all
the time.

JULIE. But you needn't stay there all day, too.

MARIE. Oh, yes. I sit near the cashier's cage, read the pa-
pers, keep an eye on the waiters and drink in the bustle
and excitement of the great city.

JULIE. And what about the children?

MARIE. You know what modern families are like. Par-
ents scarcely ever see their children these days. The four

girls are with their governess, the three boys with their tutor.

LOUISE. [*Left of* JULIE.] Auntie, dear, do stay and eat with us.

MARIE. [*Importantly.*] Impossible today, dear child, impossible. Perhaps some other time. Come, Mr. Beifeld.

JULIE. Since when do you call your husband Mister?

WOLF. I'd rather she did, dear lady. When we used to be very familiar we quarreled all the time. Now we are formal with each other and get along like society folk. I kiss your hand, dear lady.

JULIE. Good-bye, Wolf.

MARIE. Adieu, my dear. [*They embrace.*] Adieu, my dear child.

LOUISE. Good-bye, Aunt Marie. Good-bye, Uncle Wolf.

[WOLF *and* MARIE *exit Right.*]

JULIE. [*Closes gate.*] You can get the soup now, Louise dear.

[LOUISE *goes into the house and reënters with the soup. They sit at the table on porch.*]

LOUISE. [*Above table.*] Mother, is it true we're not going to work at the jute factory any more?

JULIE. [*Right of table.*] Yes, dear.

LOUISE. Where then?

JULIE. Uncle Wolf has gotten us a place in a big establishment where they make all kinds of fittings for cafés

We're to make big curtains, you know, the kind they hang in the windows, with lettering on them.

LOUISE. It'll be nicer there than at the jute factory.

JULIE. Yes, dear. The work isn't as dirty and pays better, too. A poor widow like your mother is lucky to get it.

[*They eat. Heavenly MUSIC is heard.* LILIOM *and the two* HEAVENLY POLICEMEN *appear at the Right. The* POLICEMEN *pause a moment, then exit. MUSIC stops.* LILIOM *stands there alone a moment, then crosses slowly and pauses at the gate. He is dressed as he was on the day of his death. He is very pale, but otherwise unaltered.* JULIE, *at the table, has her back to him.* LOUISE *sits facing the audience.*]

LILIOM. Good day.

LOUISE. Good day.

JULIE. [*Not looking at him.*] Another beggar! What is it you want, my poor man?

LILIOM. Nothing.

JULIE. We have no money to give, but if you care for a plate of soup— [LOUISE *goes into the house.*] Have you come far today?

LILIOM. Yes—very far.

JULIE. Are you tired?

LILIOM. Very tired.

JULIE. Over there at the gate is a stone. Sit down and rest. My daughter is bringing you the soup.

[LOUISE *comes out of the house.*]

LILIOM. [*Rapturously.*] Is that your daughter?

JULIE. Yes.

LILIOM. [*To* LOUISE.] You are the daughter?

LOUISE. Yes, sir.

LILIOM. A fine, healthy girl. [*At gate. Takes the soup plate from her with one hand, while with the other he touches her arm.*]

LOUISE. [*Draws back quickly. Crosses to* JULIE.] Mother!

JULIE. What, my child?

LOUISE. The man tried to take me by the arm.

JULIE. Nonsense! You only imagined it, dear. The poor, hungry man has other things to think about than fooling with young girls. Sit down and eat your soup. [*They eat.*]

LILIOM. [*Sits on bench Right Center. Eats, too, but keeps looking at them.*] You work at the factory, eh?

JULIE. Yes.

LILIOM. Your daughter, too?

LOUISE. Yes.

LILIOM. And your husband?

JULIE. [*After a pause.*] I have no husband. I'm a widow.

LILIOM. A widow?

JULIE. Yes.

LILIOM. Your husband—I suppose he's been dead a long

time. [JULIE *does not answer.*] I say—has your husband been dead a long time?

JULIE. A long time.

LILIOM. What did he die of?

[JULIE *is silent.*]

LOUISE. No one knows. He went to America to work and he died there—in the hospital. Poor Father, I never knew him.

LILIOM. He went to America?

LOUISE. Yes, before I was born.

LILIOM. To America?

JULIE. Why do you ask so many questions? Did you know him, perhaps?

LILIOM. [*Puts the plate down on bench.*] Heaven knows! I've known so many people. Maybe I knew him, too.

JULIE. Well, if you knew him, leave him and us in peace with your questions. He went to America and died there. That's all there is to tell.

LILIOM. All right. All right. Don't be angry with me. I didn't mean any harm.

[*There is a pause.*]

LOUISE. My father was a very handsome man.

JULIE. Don't talk so much.

LOUISE. Did I say anything—?

LILIOM. Surely the little orphan can say *that* about her father.

LOUISE. My father could juggle so beautifully with three ivory balls that people used to advise him to go on the stage.

JULIE. Who told you that?

LOUISE. Uncle Wolf.

LILIOM. Who is that?

LOUISE. Mr. Wolf Beifeld, who owns the Café Sorrento.

LILIOM. The one who used to be a porter?

JULIE. [*Astonished.*] Do you know him, too? It seems that you know all Budapest.

LILIOM. Wolf Beifeld is a long way from being all Budapest. But I do know a lot of people. Why shouldn't I know Wolf Beifeld?

LOUISE. He was a friend of my father.

JULIE. He was not his friend. No one was.

LILIOM. You speak of your husband so sternly.

JULIE. What's that to you? Doesn't it suit you? I can speak of my husband any way I like. It's nobody's business but mine.

LILIOM. Certainly, certainly—it's your own business.

[*Takes up his soup plate again. All three eat.*]

LOUISE. [*To* JULIE.] Perhaps he knew Father, too.

JULIE. Ask him, if you like.

LOUISE. [*Crosses to* LILIOM. *He stands up.*] Did you know my father? [LILIOM *nods.* LOUISE *addresses her mother.*] Yes, he knew him.

JULIE. [*Rises. Does not look at him.*] You knew Andreas Zavoczki?

LILIOM. Liliom? Yes.

LOUISE. Was he really a very handsome man?

LILIOM. I wouldn't exactly say handsome.

LOUISE. [*Confidently.*] But he was an awfully good man, wasn't he?

LILIOM. He wasn't so good, either. As far as I know he was what they called a clown, a barker in a carousel.

LOUISE. [*Pleased.*] Did he tell funny jokes?

LILIOM. Lots of 'em. And he sang funny songs, too.

LOUISE. In the carousel?

LILIOM. Yes—but he was something of a bully, too. He'd fight anyone. He even hit your dear little mother.

JULIE. [*Half turns.*] That's a lie.

LILIOM. It's true.

JULIE. Aren't you ashamed to tell the child such awful things about her father? Get out of here, you shameless liar. Eats our soup and our bread and has the impudence to slander our dead!

LILIOM. I didn't mean—I—

JULIE. What right have you to tell lies to the child? Take that plate, Louise, and let him be on his way. If he wasn't such a hungry-looking beggar, I'd put him out myself.

[LOUISE *takes the plate out of his hand.*]

LILIOM. So he didn't hit you?

JULIE. No, never. He was always good to me.

LOUISE. [*Whispers.*] Did he tell funny stories, too?

LILIOM. Yes, and *such* funny ones.

JULIE. Don't speak to him any more. In God's name, go.

LOUISE. In God's name. [*Crosses to Left of gate and closes it.*]

[JULIE *resumes her seat at the table and eats.*]

LILIOM. If you please, Miss—I have a pack of cards in my pocket. And if you like, I'll show you some tricks that'll make you split your sides laughing. [LOUISE *holds* LILIOM's *plate in her left hand. With her right she reaches out and holds the garden gate shut.*] Let me in, just a little way, Miss, and I'll do the tricks for you.

LOUISE. Go, in God's name, and let us be. Why are you making those ugly faces?

LILIOM. Don't chase me away, Miss; let me come in for just a minute—just for a minute—just long enough to let me show you something pretty, something wonderful. [*Opens the gate.*] Miss, I've something to give you. [*Takes from his pocket a big red handkerchief in which is wrapped a glittering star from Heaven. He looks furtively about him to make sure that the* POLICE *are not watching.*]

LOUISE. What's that?

LILIOM. Pst! A star! [*With a gesture he indicates that he has stolen it out of the sky.*]

JULIE. [*Sternly.*] Don't take anything from him. He's

probably stolen it somewhere. [*To* LILIOM.] In God's name, be off with you.

LOUISE. Yes, be off with you. Be off. [*She slams the gate.*]

LILIOM. Miss—please, Miss—I've got to do something good—or—do something good—a good deed·—

LOUISE. [*Pointing with her right hand.*] That's the way out.

LILIOM. Miss—

LOUISE. Get out!

LILIOM. Miss! [*Looks up at her suddenly and slaps her extended hand, so that the slap resounds loudly.*]

LOUISE. Mother! [*Looks dazedly at* LILIOM, *who bows his head dismayed, forlorn.*]

[JULIE *rises and looks at* LILIOM *in astonishment. There is a long pause.*]

JULIE. [*Comes over to them slowly.*] What's the matter here?

LOUISE. [*Back to Left a bit. Bewildered, does not take her eyes off* LILIOM.] Mother—the man—he hit me—on the hand—hard—I heard the sound of it—but it didn't hurt—mother—it didn't hurt—it was like a caress—as if he had just touched my hand tenderly. [*She hides behind* JULIE.]

[LILIOM *sulkily raises his head and looks at* JULIE.]

JULIE. [*Softly.*] Go, my child. Go into the house. Go.

LOUISE. [*Going.*] But Mother—I'm afraid—it sounded so loud— [*Weepingly.*] And it didn't hurt at all—just as if he'd—kissed my hand instead—Mother! [*She hides her face.*]

JULIE. Go in, my child, go in.

[LOUISE *goes slowly into the house.* JULIE *watches her until she has disappeared, then turns slowly to* LILIOM.]

JULIE. You struck my child.

LILIOM. Yes—I struck her.

JULIE. Is that what you came for, to strike my child?

LILIOM. No—I didn't come for that—but I did strike her —and now I'm going back.

JULIE. In the name of the Lord Jesus, who are you?

LILIOM. [*Simply.*] A poor, tired beggar who came a long way and who was hungry. And I took your soup and bread and I struck your child. Are you angry with me?

JULIE. [*Her hand on her heart; fearfully, wonderingly.*] Jesus protect me—I don't understand it—I'm *not* angry —not angry at all—

[LILIOM *turns away, going upstage to the wall, his back to audience.*]

JULIE. [*Not looking at him.*] Louise! [LOUISE *comes out of the house. Crosses to* JULIE *Left Center.*] Sit down, dear, we'll finish eating.

LOUISE. Has he gone?

JULIE. Yes. Why don't you eat, dear?

WARN CURTAIN

LOUISE. What has happened, Mother?

JULIE. Nothing, my child. [*Heavenly MUSIC is heard. The* HEAVENLY POLICEMEN *appear Right. They point off and* LILIOM *walks slowly off at Right. The* FIRST POLICEMAN *makes a deploring gesture and* BOTH *follow* LILIOM *slowly off at Right. STOP MUSIC.*]

LOUISE. Mother, dear, why won't you tell me?

JULIE. What is there to tell you, child? [*Crosses and sits on bench Right Center.*] Nothing has happened. We were peacefully eating, and a beggar came who talked of bygone days, and then I thought of your father.

LOUISE. My father?

JULIE. Your father—Liliom.

[*There is a pause.*]

LOUISE. Mother—tell me—has it ever happened to you —has anyone ever hit you—without hurting you in the least?

JULIE. Yes, my child. It has happened to me, too.

[*There is a pause.*]

LOUISE. Is it possible for someone to hit you—hard like that—real loud and hard—and not hurt you at all?

JULIE. It is possible, dear—that someone may beat you and beat you and beat you,—and not hurt you at all.—

[*There is a pause. Nearby an organ-grinder has stopped. The music of his ORGAN begins.*]

THE CURTAIN FALLS

PROPERTY PLOT

PROLOGUE

Calliope
Red carnation (GIRL)
Coffee and rolls (MRS. MUSKAT)
Weights (STRONG MAN)
Punch and Judy figures
Cigarette (LILIOM)
Money
Noise makers, balloons, etc.

SCENE I

Blossoms

SCENE II

Camera
Screen
Tripod
Firewood ⎫
Water pot ⎬ (MOTHER HOLLUNDER)
Cup of coffee (JULIE)
Purse (MRS. MUSKAT)
Coins (in purse)
Shawl (on couch)

SCENE III

Large butcher knife ⎫
Pack of cards ⎬ (LILIOM)

Photo plate (MOTHER HOLLUNDER)

SCENE IV

Pack of cards ⎫
Large butcher knife ⎬ (LILIOM)
Coins ⎭
Coins ⎫
Pocket knife ⎬ (FICSUR)
Leather bag on strap ⎫
Revolver ⎬ (LINZMAN)
Revolver (FIRST POLICEMAN)
Ambulance bell (offstage)

SCENE V

Candle (off up Right)
Bible (on table)
Fountain pen (WOLF)
Printed form (DOCTOR)

SCENE VI

Book (MAGISTRATE's bench)
Notebook (FIRST POLICEMAN)
Cigarettes, matches (GUARD)

SCENE VII

3 soup plates ⎫
Bread ⎬ (on table)
Eating utensils ⎭
Star (LILIOM)
Cigar (WOLF)
Serving bowl (off Left)

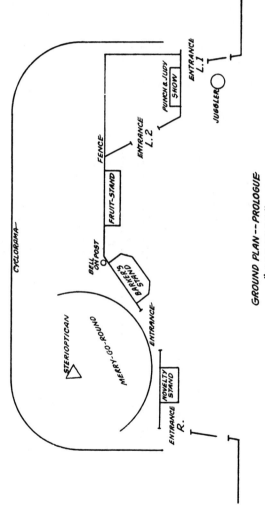

GROUND PLAN -- PROLOGUE
"LILIOM"

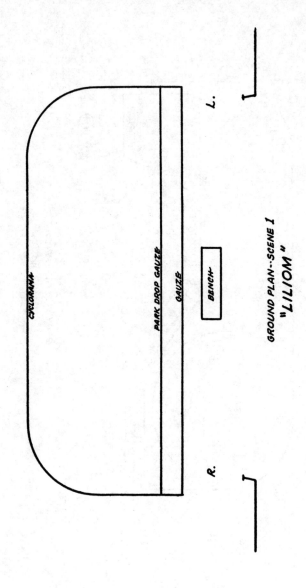

GROUND PLAN--SCENE 1
"LILIOM"

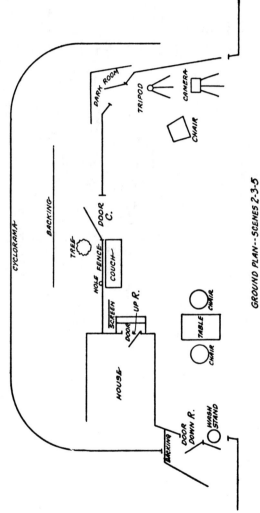

GROUND PLAN--SCENES 2-3-5
"LILIOM"

GROUND PLAN--SCENE 4
"LILIOM"

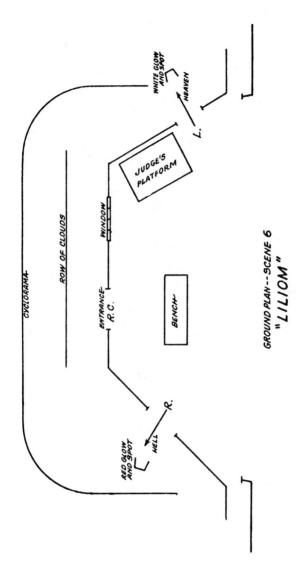

GROUND PLAN--SCENE 6
"LILIOM"

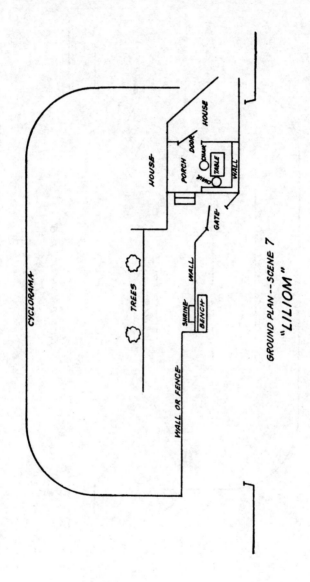

GROUND PLAN -- SCENE 7
"LILIOM"